# I'M NOT GONNA LIE

# I'M NOT GONNA LIE

# GONNA LIE

And Other Lies You Tell When You Turn 50

---

# GEORGE LOPEZ

with Alan Eisenstock

A CELEBRA BOOK

Celebra
Published by the Penguin Group
Penguin Group (USA) Inc., 375 Hudson Street,
New York, New York 10014, USA

USA | Canada | UK | Ireland | Australia
New Zealand | India | South Africa | China
Penguin Books Ltd., Registered Offices: 80 Strand, London WC2R 0RL,
England
For more information about the Penguin Group visit penguin.com

First published by Celebra,
a division of Penguin Group (USA) Inc.

First Printing, May 2013
10  9  8  7  6  5  4  3  2  1

All photographs: Matt Hoyle

LIBRARY OF CONGRESS CATALOGING-IN-PUBLICATION DATA:

Lopez, George, 1961–
  I'm not gonna lie, and other lies you tell when you turn 50/George Lopez,
with Alan Eisenstock.
    p. cm.
  ISBN 978-0-451-41710-7 (hardback)
1. Lopez, George, 1961–  2. Comedians—United States—Biography.
3. Television actors and actresses—United States—Biography.
4. Hispanic-American comedians—Biography.
5. Hispanic-American television actors and actresses—Biography.
6. Aging—Humor.  I. Eisenstock, Alan.  II. Title.
  PN2287.L633A3 2013
  792.702'8092—dc23      2012045899
  [B]

Set in New Baskerville
Designed by Spring Hoteling

To my daughter, Mayan,
the light of my life.

# CONTENTS

# CONTENTS

# I'M NOT GONNA LIE

# INTRODUCTION
# COUNTING FAIRWAYS

I did it!

I hit the number.

Unbelievable.

I turned fifty!

Without a doubt, my biggest birthday ever.

I'm not lying: Reaching fifty meant a lot to me.

For starters, it meant I wasn't dead.

Most people take turning fifty for granted. Not me. I nearly died when I was forty-four. Kidney disease. I survived that, but it was touch-and-go all the way. In fact, I'd call my forties a touch-and-go decade. I was blessed with a lot of success, including an ALMA Special Achievement Award for television, two Grammy Award nominations, and a sitcom that ran for six years. But I also got a kidney transplant, went through a divorce, and had two TV shows canceled. I'm not sure what stressed me out the most. Probably the divorce. It was not what you would call amicable.

So, yes, at times my forties were rough. But if I had to pick the one decade when I was the most nervous, that would be my first, also known as my childhood. Talk about a shaky start. My father took one look at me and left. That's not true. He waited two whole months and then he left. It took my mother longer. She gave it a shot, but she was young and troubled and not fit to be a mom, so she handed me off to my grandparents when I was ten.

Growing up, I lived in constant fear of death: I was deathly afraid of pissing off my grandmother. For some reason, she was always agitated. No matter what she was doing, morning, noon, or night, if I approached her and started to talk to her, she would say:

"What now?"

That was her catchphrase. It didn't matter what I said to her.

"Hi, Grandma."

"What now?"

Never "Yes? What is it? What can I do for you?"

No. She'd say, "What now?"

And I would get intimidated and say, "I forgot."

Then she'd say, "Well, if you forgot, it must have been a lie. Because you never forget the truth."

My grandmother was right. So that's why I'm not gonna lie. Anymore. Not at my age. I don't have that good a memory.

Thinking back to my childhood, I realize my grandmother did not make my life easy, because everything with her was a labor.

"Grandma?"

"What now?"

"Can I have two dollars?"

"For what?"

"Um . . . just . . . I need two dollars."

"For *what?*"

"To buy a car."

I wish I had been smart enough or brave enough to have said something like that, but I wasn't. I can pretend that I was this fast—

"Grandma, can I have a dollar?"

"For what?"

"To go to college."

Yes, I walked on eggshells a lot in my childhood, but I had good times, too. But even though I felt the most nervous in my early years, my worst decade was definitely the years forty through forty-nine. I was very glad to see that decade come to an end. I spent my whole forty-ninth year waiting for the calendar to flip to that magic number.

In fact, the closer I came to turning fifty, the better I felt. It was almost like a cloud lifting. Sure, I experienced a little bit of dread and anxiety. But mostly I felt excited. Then about a week before my birthday a sense of calm came over me. I knew I was gonna make it. I was so ready.

The night before the big day, I flew to Las Vegas and checked into my favorite hotel. I had a nice quiet dinner with a couple of friends and turned in early. I was so excited about my party I couldn't sleep. I tried counting sheep, but that never works. I always seem to conjure up these big, nasty, belligerent sheep. I tell them to jump slowly over the imaginary fence and they refuse. They glare at me. That first sheep looks about the size of Babe the Blue Ox. He looks at me and smoke starts pouring out of his snout, and he says to me in Spanish, "Fuck that, *puto.*" Then he rounds up all the other sheep into this sheep gang and they charge at me, crashing right through the fence.

Forget sheep. I needed something more soothing.

Cars. I love cars. I closed my eyes and thought about all the cars I've owned in my life.

I remembered one of my first cars, an old clunker that sounded like it had emphysema every time you hit the gas. That was only one of its quirks. This car made me crazy. For one thing, it never turned off when you turned it off. It just kept going, like it was alive. It growled and shrieked, and the hood shook as if the car were having a seizure. I'd lift up the hood and look down at the engine, nodding and pointing as if I knew exactly what I was do- ing, even though I had absolutely no clue. Other guys would gather around and they'd all nod and point at the engine, too. They didn't know anything, either. We'd just all nod and point at the carburetor and battery and hoses like we were a pit crew. Eventually, the car would just stop on its own. We'd all walk away, still nodding like we fixed the thing, saying a bunch of made-up car talk.

"Yeah, see, I knew that would happen. Air gets caught in the air conductor valves and causes the engine cap to virtisify. . . ."

"Definitely. Plus the igniter switch deadens the pres- sure. . . ."

"Oh, absolutely. Plus a gas bubble fornicates the air hose. . . ."

"That will mess you up."

The car had other issues, too. It played only one ra- dio station—all polka music—because the knobs kept falling off. Oh, and the side mirrors were held on with electrical tape. And the locks didn't work, either, so whenever I got in I was sure I'd find some crazy bat-shit guy living in the backseat.

You know what? Forget counting cars to fall asleep.

Then it hit me.

The perfect thing.

Golf courses.

I decided to picture myself walking down all the beautiful courses I'd ever played. I've played most of the best courses in the world. I knew this would work.

I settled into the king-size bed in my suite in Vegas, got really comfortable, closed my eyes, and pictured historic St. Andrews in Scotland, site of several British Opens and one of the most gorgeous courses ever. Some people call St. Andrews the "home of golf." I can believe it. In my mind, I saw the entire breathtaking course, every hole, imagining myself strolling down those gently rolling green fairways, each one bordered by castles. I saw myself walking onto the first tee with my buddy, mentor, and golf companion, the great Lee Trevino. I felt totally relaxed. I stabbed my ball and tee into the grass, stepped back, and caught Lee's eye. He was standing off to the side. He grinned and nodded. I smiled back. I took a practice swing, stepped up to my ball, took a breath, exhaled, and swung.

*Thwack.*

The ball shot off my driver and rocketed right into the middle of the fairway.

Oh, man. There is nothing sweeter than the feeling

you get when you hit a good golf shot. It's better than sex. At least, I think it's better than sex. I'm fifty. I don't remember.

After I hit that drive, I looked over at Lee. He gave me two thumbs up. He's seventy-three, wise, and full of life. I picked up my tee, slid my driver into my bag, and Lee and I walked down the fairway through the hazy Scottish sunlight and into a cool, craggy shadow cast by a medieval castle. We walked for a good fifty yards before Lee finally spoke.

"Golf or comedy?" he said. "If you had to choose one, which would it be?"

I didn't hesitate for a second. "Golf."

"You sure?"

"Absolutely. Now, if you were Richard Pryor—"

I took two more steps down the fairway at St. Andrews and drifted off into a deep sleep.

When I woke up, I was fifty.

Everything seemed different. The air seemed fresher, the light in the room more vibrant. I lifted my hand and felt a tiny pulse of energy shooting through me like a charge of electricity. I felt wiser, more distinguished, more intelligent. Fifty was going to be great!

I lounged around in bed until noon, kinglike. I got up, slipped on my robe, padded to the minibar, and poured myself a birthday cocktail—cranberry juice and vodka. This is the perfect morning pick-me-up. You cleanse and get buzzed at the same time. Some bartenders call this cocktail "Sex on the Beach," which is one place I would never have sex, because I'm a clean freak and I hate the idea of sand all up in my *culo.*

I drained my drink and started to get ready for my big day. That night I was hosting a birthday party for twenty of my closest friends from the old neighborhood. I couldn't wait to see them and celebrate. This party was very special to me, because I don't usually celebrate my birthdays.

Growing up, my birthday was no big deal. It was just another day. And a birthday party? Nope. Never had a birthday party. Ever. Not one.

On my birthday, my grandmother and grandfather would say, "Hey, happy birthday." That was it. Celebration over. No cake, no candles, no balloons, no hats, no pony ride, no clown, and no bouncy thing, unless you count when my grandmother knocked me down and I hit the floor and bounced right back up.

And no presents.

If I was out shopping with my grandmother anytime during the month or two before and I saw a toy or a jacket that I wanted, I'd say, "Can I have that?"

She'd say, "All right, but that's for your birthday. Make sure you remember that when your birthday comes. You want it?"

I'd scrunch my forehead and think about this carefully. I felt like I was on a game show. "Okay, yes; wait, no; I don't know; okay, *yes,* I'll take it."

"Good. Now I don't have to buy you nothing for your birthday. Cross that off."

So when I turned fifty, I finally decided to throw myself

a party. I wanted to mark the day with my best friends from my childhood, some of whom I hadn't seen in thirty years. This seemed like a great idea when I thought of it.

Uh, no.

Big mistake.

I don't know what happened.

Those guys got *old*.

One guy who used to have hair like Tony Orlando's turned completely bald. He looked Asian. I kept staring at him, thinking, "How the hell did that happen?" Another guy had a bad back. He could barely walk. We had to help him out of his chair every time he got up. Another guy was so heavy he wore suspenders and a belt to keep all of his jiggling fat inside his clothes.

"Really?" I said to myself. "At fifty? Damn."

The worst was my best friend, who, as a kid, was the neighborhood stud. I can't explain what happened to him except that it was scary. He looked like an aunt. A Mexican aunt.

I knew I didn't look as young as I once did, but these guys looked like hell. I didn't look like them, did I? I wanted someone to tell me I looked great, but nobody said anything. Maybe they couldn't see, either.

As the party went on, I thought, "I'm fifty, but I can't have aged that much." And then I whispered a prayer: "I know I'm not the most religious person in the world, but please don't make me look like an old Mexican lady."

We had a great time. We shared a lot of laughs and memories, and shed a few tears. Then, when it was time to call it a night, they all went into the same room. Twenty fat, bald, ugly guys and a Mexican aunt sharing one room with twin beds. Damn. I went back to my room, thinking, "I grew up with guys who can't even afford a hotel room in Vegas? They practically give those rooms away."

When I woke up the next morning, my world changed. Everything felt like it was going downhill. It began when I realized, I'm no longer fifty. I am now *in* my fifties. This is horrible.

I'm fifty going on fifty-one.

The run-up to fifty wasn't that bad.

Turning fifty sucked.

It was like I'd arrived at the door of this hot new club, Studio 51, and I'm standing outside nervously, and the bouncer says, "I don't know if I can let you in." And I peer inside, and I say, "Hey, this place is nice. I'd really like to get in. I know people in there. Come on. I'm George Lopez. Let me in."

The bouncer looks me over and says, "Okay, you can go in."

I stride in like I own the place. Feels great at first, but the deeper I get inside the club, the darker it gets. My legs feel wobbly, my face starts to sweat, my hands feel clammy, my vision gets blurry, and my heart sinks.

I'm not gonna lie.

I was fine with fifty.

But being *in* my fifties?

That could be the end of the road.

# POP GOES THE . . . WAIT, WAS THAT ME?

**I'M** gonna tell you the truth.

I lied. A lot.

Okay, that's a lie.

I lied all the time.

I lied to survive. And I lied because it seemed as if nobody wanted to hear the truth. I just told people what they wanted to hear. I also lied by withholding information, which is another kind of lie. Here's one of those.

Once, during the dark days of my marriage, I decided to surprise my wife with a bottle of champagne. Things had been sort of unraveling, and I thought a romantic evening might help us turn the ship around. I didn't know that by then the ship had already crashed and was taking on water like the *Titanic*, but . . .

Anyway, to enhance the romance, I popped a little blue pill. Yes. I took a Viagra. This was a really big deal for me, because philosophically I'm opposed to unnatural male enhancement. But I really wanted this evening to be perfect.

Then, before I even uncorked the champagne, we got into a huge screaming fight and I stormed upstairs with a boner the size of a baseball bat.

Great.

I'm upstairs with a huge hard-on and nobody to offer me relief.

Have you read the label on the Viagra bottle? I stared at it in horror. I was about to have a boner for four hours. Really? Four *hours*? What was I supposed to do for four hours in this condition? I couldn't leave the house. I couldn't phone out-call massage. My wife was downstairs, and I was betting she was not gonna understand. Or be sympathetic. All I could think of was, "How great is this? I take a pill, we get into a fight, I get a massive hard-on, and all I got up here is basic cable and DVDs of my sitcom."

**WHEN I TURNED FIFTY, I ASKED MYSELF A QUESTION: "DO YOU WANT TO BE A LIAR YOUR WHOLE LIFE? DO YOU WANT YOUR LIFE TO BE ONE BIG LIE?"**

It also says on the bottle that if your erection lasts for more than four hours you should seek medical assistance. Really? I'm not calling my doctor. He wears thick wraparound glasses that make him look like a welder and has hair the size of an Afro coming out of both ears. If I need to call somebody to finish this off, I'm gonna text my wife downstairs and ask, "Hey, is your sister home?"

I should've been honest. I should've said, "Look, I know we had a terrible fight, but I took a Viagra and I need some relief. Guzzle some champagne, close your eyes, and pretend I'm Benjamin Bratt. I need *help*!"

When I turned fifty, I asked myself a question: "Do you want to be a liar your whole life? Do you want your life to be one big lie?"

No.

Since my birthday party, I've been truthful. Instead of accommodating people all the time, I tell people what I like and what I don't. I've undergone a transformation. I've become more comfortable with myself. I like my life.

And here's the biggest surprise: I like telling the truth. It's a total relief. Lying was like swimming in a muddy river. I want to swim in clear water. If I'm going to swim in muddy water, I'm going to dirty it myself. I'm losing track of my point. I just know that all this talk about rivers and water is making me want to find a bathroom.

**SO,** okay, now I'm being real.

You know what I said about being fine with turning fifty?

I lied.

I hate it.

I *haaate* it.

I suddenly realize that I'm old. What's worse is that I feel old. I know that from now on I'm gonna be in more pain than usual. Why? I'm *fifty*.

It happened already.

First thing this morning.

I got out of bed and something popped. Pop. Just like that. *Pop.* I could not figure out where it came from. I stopped in my tracks and looked around. Where the hell did that pop come from? I heard the pop, all right, but from where? It came from somewhere out there. There was a shot—I heard it—but nobody knows where it came from. It was like the grassy knoll.

It was so strange. Nothing hurt. I patted myself all over, searched for a bone or a knuckle or something out of place or sticking out or not where it should be, and I couldn't find anything. I took another step and it happened again—

*Pop!*

What the hell? I'm standing in the middle of the room, frozen in place, my eyes passing over the room like searchlights, like I'm looking for somebody who broke into the house, and I know the pop came from me, because there's nobody else in here, and I say, "So that's how this goes? I turn fifty and my body goes pop just *because?*"

Life after fifty. It's miserable. And it's only beginning.

And—hold on—did it take me longer to get upright than it did when I was forty-nine? I think so. I'm definitely moving slower. The difference of one day felt like twenty years.

And then I had my first over-fifty realization—well, besides you go *pop* for no reason.

When you turn fifty, everything changes—the way you think, the way you look, the way you approach your day. Little things become big things. Stuff that never used to matter—crap you never even noticed—suddenly becomes important. What's up is down; what's down is up—hell, everything is messed up. You have no choice except to deal with it. You have to adjust.

For example, now when I go to work, I have to plan which car I'm gonna take. That was never an issue before. Now I think, "I can't take that car because it sits too low. I'll never get out of that damn car."

I can't pull up to my office looking all cool in my Porsche. I can't do that anymore. It's too risky. I don't want to have to call security to send over the Jaws of Life to lift me out of my car.

I'm also much more conscious of time. I've started to slow down, to take everything easy. Time itself seems to rocket by. When I was younger, I never thought about how fast the day went. I wanted time to fly. I wanted to be old enough to be on my own, to start my own life, to escape. Now I don't mind waiting. When people get annoyed and say to me, "Hey, I've been waiting for twenty minutes," I want to tell them to chill out. Appreciate the time you have. Enjoy each minute. Time is precious.

I also stopped saying, "I'll see you later." At my age there may not be a later.

There's also more pressure on me to look younger, because my show is still on TV all the time in syndication. In the show, I'm in my forties. People think of me as that age, as if I'm frozen in time. I also look younger because I have all my hair.

And, okay, keep this between us. . . .

I dye it.

I have to.

Couple reasons. First, my hair started going gray in my mid-thirties. I first noticed specks of gray when I was doing stand-up. One night, the spotlight hit me and it looked like I had tinsel in my hair. I couldn't believe it. I aged twenty years during that one set.

A short time after that, I was signing autographs for this kid who was about eight years old. The kid stared at me, made a face like something near him smelled, and said, "Hey, your hair is gray." I laughed, rubbed the top of his head affectionately, and thought, "You little shit."

But he was right. I was looking and feeling a lot older than I was. I didn't want people staring at me, going, "Is that George Lopez? No. That's not George Lopez. It sort of looks like him, but that guy is much older. Let's ask him. Hey, old guy, you're not George Lopez, are you?"

I admit that going prematurely gray and having little kids tell me that I looked old bummed me out. The only thing that made me feel better was that they got a wax figure of me at Madame Tussauds. At least that wax George Lopez will be forty-five forever. From now on I plan to go in there every year, take a picture, see how far I'm getting from looking like that, and adjust.

When I look around me—especially in Hollywood, where everybody is desperately trying to look young and usually failing—I rarely see guys my age who can pull it off. One exception.

Pee-wee Herman.

I saw him on Broadway and he looked terrific. I'm sure he was funny, but I don't know for sure, because I was too distracted by how he looked. He looked exactly the same. It was inspiring. He'd gained a few pounds, but not many. He knows he has an image to protect, so he's devoted himself to looking the way he always did—same suits, same shoes, same high voice. He's my new idol. I want to stay as young as Pee-wee.

So, the first thing I did was dye my hair.

Next, I became very conscious of the clothes I wear.

You have to be careful when you turn fifty.

President Obama and I are the same age, but he wears mom jeans. He really should think about a different look. I've noticed some gray in his hair, too. I'm not saying he should go for a total dye job like me, but he might want to consider some highlights. He should be careful. He doesn't want to look like the guys at my party, especially the Mexican aunt.

I realize I'll have to change my look eventually. Because I know that at some point that same little kid is going to look at me and say, "What's that old man doing wearing those PRPS?"

For now, though, I can carry it off. But you have to be aware of a delicate balance. Like the other day, I saw an old black man wearing Velcro shoes, high ankle socks, and this black plastic thing that looked like he cut two holes in a trash bag. *No.* You cannot do that. You must keep a constant watchful eye on yourself. You can't go from looking good in jeans one day to suddenly wearing black socks and sandals.

Yes, how you look matters. And as you get older, you have to be on alert twenty-four/seven. You cannot let it slide. I was walking in New York and I saw this lady around my age crossing the street. It was a brutally hot day and she was wearing a ski parka. She looked like a Hershey's Kiss: skinny at the top and then she widened out like a lemon drop. Smoking a cigarette. Struggling to walk. Limping. I wanted to run up to her and say, "Lady, no, you can't walk around like this. Lose the cigarette and the parka, and walk better."

I will tell you this right now: No matter what happens to me, I will not accept a limp.

I won't do it. I will not accept it. I'll do something to fix it. I will figure out a way to walk better. I'll put some cardboard in my shoe. I will do whatever I have to. You cannot drag your leg across the street. It's mind over matter. You have to say to yourself, "I'm not limping today. I'm just not gonna limp. Not happening."

And you cannot use a cane. Forget that. Nobody can make a cane look good. Except maybe Mr. Peanut. He pulls it off. Actually, he pulls off the very rare fashion triple play—monocle, cane, and top hat. Mr. Peanut is a bad dude. Yes, I'm in awe of Mr. Peanut.

The only other person who could pull off walking with a cane was Evel Knievel. That's the only way I'd use a cane—if I had one that belonged to Evel Knievel. A real one. One of the ones from his collection. Maybe I could talk to his family. I bet they'd gift me a cane. If someone from the Evel Knievel family is reading this, I'm serious. I would accept one of Evel's canes and I would walk with it proudly. I respect the man. He broke every bone in his body—doing some pretty outrageous and stupid stuff—but he walked away, limping only a little bit, supporting himself on those cool canes. Which he used to fill with Wild Turkey. Allegedly. You have to love that.

After all he went through, I have to admit that Evel

had a limp I appreciate. And when it comes to medical procedures, I've had more things done to me than anyone. I've replaced all my teeth, had stents, surgeries, transplants. I'm the Evel Knievel of comedy. You bet I'd take one of his canes.

I try like crazy to take care of myself, but, to be honest, that's not going so well.

You've heard the expression "My body is a temple"?

Mine is more like a storage unit.

I keep a ton of medicine in there, because I have to. I put in some things that I should've gotten rid of a while ago, and I have a whole bunch of junk that I shoved in there that I forgot about. I know this. I have to get over to my storage unit soon and clean all that out. After you turn fifty, you have to be very careful about what you put into your storage-unit body.

**YOU'VE HEARD THE EXPRESSION "MY BODY IS A TEMPLE"? MINE IS MORE LIKE A STORAGE UNIT.**

I try.

I monitor everything I drink and eat. I don't eat a lot, and I do my best to eat right. For one thing, I'm not a vegetarian. I tried that once and I passed out in the street. Keeled over. Bang. I took a nosedive right into traffic. Caused a Sigalert. By the way, I love to watch that hot blond traffic reporter, who's somehow on every channel, announce in her ditzy, sexy voice that there's been a Sig-alert. I have no idea what a Sigalert is, but I know it's bad. I picture a long-haired maniac named Sig running na-ked down Ventura Boulevard screaming and waving a machete.

I lasted being a vegetarian for only a few weeks. I ate nothing but bean-and-cheese burritos, salads, toast, rice, and noodles. That was my entire diet. I wasn't vegan. You can't do that. It's too much. Your breath smells like an ass.

There I was in the middle of the day and my world started to spin. I had a salad for lunch, dressing on the side, no bread, a cup of tea—very healthy—and I was leaving this restaurant, a famous vegetarian place in Hol-lywood—I forget the name, Bubba's Fat Flabby Bouncing Belly, or Real Food Tastes Like Cardboard Daily, or the Golden Temple of Conscious Colon Cleansing, some-thing like that. I stepped off the curb, took two steps, felt light-headed, my knees buckled, and I went down. If only I'd had an Evel Knievel cane, I could've braced myself.

So, yes, I cannot be a vegetarian. I get woozy. I could barely make it out of the restaurant.

Now, it could've been the weed.

I suppose that's a possibility.

Sure, I get high. I have to. Doctor's orders. That's right. My doctor told me to. It's medicinal. I have my medical marijuana card. I carry it with me at all times, right between my license and my condoms. When some-body asks for two forms of ID, I pull all this shit out and watch their faces turn red and their eyes bug out. It's great.

The truth is, in my condition, I don't know where I'd be without weed. Weed saved my ass. Pot soothes my aches and pains, relieves my stress, calms my stomach, takes away my nausea, and improves my enjoyment of Van Halen.

I liked Van Halen before my kidney disease, but now, with a little boost from medicinal marijuana, I love them. They can play anything—any riff at all—and they blow my mind. I give them a standing ovation while they tune up.

Yes, medical marijuana is a wonder drug.

I'm not gonna lie.

Weed works.

I don't like to smoke it. That's unhealthy. Like I told you, I'm careful what I put into my body. Smoking dope is bad for you.

So I eat it. Much better. And you can sneak your weed into a lot of delicious foods.

I love grass in gummy bears. Knocks me on my ass. If you don't like gummy bears, no problem. In fact, you don't have to eat grass at all. There are other possibilities. Like lotion. I love the lotion. Or the spray. You just rub it in and hang on for the ride. Consider a mutual marijuana massage with a loved one. Way better than smoking weed. One caution: Don't have her massage you first, because you will be too stoned to massage her without laughing hysterically.

So, okay, you got your lotion, spray, and gummy bears, and you also have Tootsie Rolls, barbecue sauce, popcorn, wheat chips, and, of course, brownies.

Those are amazing.

Very simple to make, too. Just get some Duncan Hines brownie mix and cook the weed right in there. Drop it right in with the butter. I don't know who came up with this idea first, but it's sheer genius. Maybe Bob Marley or Willie Nelson back in the day. I know it wasn't Duncan Hines. I don't think Duncan Hines ever said, "You know what would be great? Let's put some weed into my fudge brownies. It'll be fantastic." I doubt old Duncan was a pothead, though you never know. I know you don't see weed as one of the ingredients in the recipes on the side of the package.

Obviously, getting high at fifty serves a different purpose than it did when I was eighteen. I used to get high just to get high. It was way more fun going to a concert or a party stoned. Now I get high not just to get high, but to get through. I use weed for pain relief. I have weak joints and a lot of other residual stuff from the kidney disease. Sometimes after I've been working a long day, my body feels like one big throbbing ache. I will get high then for relief. Sad. I used to get high for fun; now I get high to function.

I actually prefer getting high to getting drunk. I started drinking when I was thirteen. I was in junior high school and a couple of friends and I crashed an older kid's party. My memory is fuzzy, but I vaguely remember this really hot girl wearing, like, nothing but a piece of string, filling and refilling my plastic cup with beer, and then handing me another cup filled with some spiked Hawaiian Punch. I started to come on to her, reached over to untie that string, shouted something really cool and funny, took two wobbly steps, and passed out. It was like being a vegetarian.

To this day, when it comes to booze, I'm a lightweight. Two beers and I'm looking for a place to lie down. With weed, I'm cool. I get quiet, reflective, and trippy. I hold my high well. I bet you'd never know I was stoned.

A few years ago in Houston, this young bellhop must've thought I was stoned, but I wasn't.

I'd played the Toyota Center and sold it out. They asked me to come back two weeks later to do a couple more shows. I was checking in at the Four Seasons downtown, my second time in two weeks, and this bell kid, who was maybe twenty-two, started gathering all my bags to take them up to my room. I called him over. "What's the biggest tip you ever got?" I said.

"Four hundred dollars," the kid said.

"Get out," I said. "Four hundred dollars? For bringing bags up to a room?"

"Yes, sir," the kid said. "That's what I got. Four hundred dollars."

I shook my head, reached into my pocket, pulled out my billfold, and peeled off five bills. "Here's five hundred," I said.

The kid's eyes got wide as plates. "Thank you, Mr. Lopez," he said. "I will take really good care of these bags."

I laughed, and he started to head up to my room.

"Hey," I said. "I want to know. Who gave you that four hundred?"

"You did," he said. "Two weeks ago."

Come to think of it, maybe I was high.

# YOU'RE NOT GONNA LIKE THE WAY IT SMELLS

**ONE** thing I hate.

People who say, "Fifty is the new thirty."

No, it's not.

Fifty is fifty.

Do the math.

Fifty is twenty years closer to death.

Even though I try to look younger, people can tell how old I am. Especially young, beautiful women. I don't know why that is.

When I was in Vegas for my birthday party, I walked into the bar in the hotel lobby and saw four young women dressed for the evening, sipping martinis. One of them noticed me, whispered to her friends, and three of them ran over to me, yelling, "It's George Lopez!"

I said, "What's going on, girls?"

A cute blonde said, "What happens in Vegas, stays in Vegas."

Annoying group giggle.

Then a brunette said, "What are you doing here?"

I said, "I'm here for my birthday. Having a little party."

I grinned and deliberately did not mention the number.

"How old are you?" the blonde said.

I shrugged.

"He's fifty," the brunette said.

How the hell did she know? Then, thinking I couldn't see them, the other two looked at each other, and, with horror, mouthed *Fifty?*

Then they made that face. All of them. At the same time. That "ewww" face.

You say "fifty" and people react like a bad smell just blew in.

**FIFTY MEANS DETERIORATION. IT'S LIKE YOU'RE A HOUSE IN DISREPAIR. YOU CAN SLAP ON A COAT OF PAINT, BUT IF THE HOUSE HAS BAD JOISTS, OR AREAS OF ROT AND MOLD, A COAT OF PAINT WILL NOT HELP.**

Once I turned fifty, it took me less than twenty-four hours to feel fifty. A black cloud descended. Fifty means deterioration. It's like you're a house in disrepair. You can slap on a coat of paint, but if the house has bad joists, or areas of rot and mold, a coat of paint will not help.

We will be discussing a lot of stuff about turning fifty—things you might want to do now, because you're approaching the end of your life, and things you should never, ever do, under any circumstances—but I want to prepare you for what will happen to you first. Some of this is not pleasant and it will be difficult to accept, but I feel it's my duty to tell you.

Here's the first thing that will happen.

You will fart for no reason.

Farts will make their appearance.

They will just come out.

You'll take a step and . . .

*Brump* . . .

Just like that.

No matter how cool you look—or try to look—farts will arrive.

I was in my car, driving to a lunch. I pulled up to the restaurant and parked. I got out and started to go inside. It was a warm L.A. day and I was dressed in slacks, a nice T-shirt—looking pretty good—and I realized I left my phone in the car. I bent over to get it and—

*Bwap, pwap, pwap.*

I jerked my head up and looked around.

"What the hell? I just bent over to get my phone. This is ridiculous."

It happens all the time now.

You walk across the room to say hi to somebody and . . .

*Prrratttt.*

Then you gotta make a noise to cover it up.

"Hah!" I say. "Hah, hah—ahem. Something's caught in my throat. *Haprrrattt.*"

A word of warning.

When you're fifty, if the room smells like shit, it's because you farted.

Finally, a piece of advice.

Try to be extra careful when you're invited to someone's house for dinner.

If you do cut one and it's loud and everybody looks at you, immediately cover your mouth and pretend that you burped.

*Bwaapppppppp.*

"Oh, excuse me. How rude. Yes, guilty as charged. Ha, *ha*. I had a little burp there, because that cauliflower casserole is so delicious."

This tactic will work, because most people consider a burp to be a compliment. But a fart, no. Although I would consider a fart a backhanded compliment.

A few months ago, I started dating a much younger woman, and after we got to know each other, she said, "You take a lot of showers."

"Yes," I said. "I do. I do because you're very young. And I'm very . . . fifty."

Also, to tell you the truth—but I couldn't admit it to her—I'm vain. And lately, I've become even more vain. Like an infinite number of times more vain.

I admit that I spend maybe a little extra time looking at myself in the mirror. I take stock. I've become very concerned about my appearance, more than ever before. I mentioned that I'm careful about what I eat. I try to eat healthy, and smaller portions than I did when I was in my thirties. I don't think the world needs another fat Mexican.

I try to control what I eat . . . and I try to stay clean.

I'll just say it.

I'm a shower fool.

If I estimate the over-under on the number of showers I take per day, I'd say a conservative number is . . . four. Yes. Four. That's about right.

What?

Too many?

I'm not sure it's enough.

Let's break it down.

A typical day. Today. It's almost noon and I've already had two showers. I'm gonna go out to lunch and then maybe play a few holes of golf. After that I'll come home and take a shower. That's three. And I will take a shower before bed. That's four.

That's my average.

I also have a steam at my house. I'll absolutely take a steam later. And I'm not gonna lie: Sometime today I will also take a bath. I count a bath as a half. I like to take a long, hot shower, but at my age I don't want to stand up that long. Too taxing. I can't stand there for twenty minutes. So I'll take a bath.

You add the steam, which is a treat, kinda like a wet, hot, sweaty dessert, plus the bath, count those each as a half, I'm up to five a day.

I don't think that's too many.

Figure it this way: You've got twenty-four hours in a day. Between sleeping and lounging around, I stay in bed for, say, nine hours. That means I'm out and about for fifteen hours a day, during which I take a shower, bath, or steam on average every three hours. What's wrong with that? I promise you that is not only normal for a person of fifty; it's *necessary*.

So, my over-fifty brothers and sisters, how do you start your day?

My advice: Begin at ground zero.

Start with a shower.

As the day goes on, work it out this way: shower, bath, shower, shower. Minimum. I'm telling you, you'll have to take a lot of showers to counteract the smell if you don't live alone, and even more so if you have a young girl-friend.

We've established that at fifty you need to emphasize cleanliness.

You also need to emphasize safety.

The first item you have to purchase, without a doubt, is a good shower mat. The other day during my second, no, third shower—wait, my fourth . . . or was it my first . . . ? Anyway, I almost fell. And I have good balance. You must accept that at fifty your body starts to go, and even doing the most basic activities, like taking a shower, can be lethal. Solution: You need a good shower mat. Everybody says that most accidents happen at home. They're right.

To old people.

People over fifty.

It makes sense that the shower is a danger zone. The floor gets wet and soapy and slippery. You're in the shower and you take one little step to grab the soap or shampoo, and—*whrrp*—your feet fly out from under you and you go down. You can't let that happen. I have a cement shower. If I go down, I'm going down hard. It could be the end. Death by hair rinse buildup on the shower floor. Not how I want my obituary to read. Do not let that happen to you. Buy a shower mat.

I've never done a survey, but I know that people have shower-mat phobia. It's a national problem. Too much bother. People don't like to use shower mats because they get dirty and moldy underneath and it's too gross to clean them. Admit it: You just throw out the old grungy one and never replace it.

Go—right now—to Kmart and buy a shower mat. We're talking about life and death. Or worse. You could fall and hit your head and *not* die. You could end up a diaper-wearing, drooling vegetable who stares at the microwave all day thinking it's the TV and calls everybody "Nana."

Buy a shower mat.

And don't believe what people say about the bottom of some tubs: that they're slip resistant. Really? They don't resist your slipping and falling on your head. And you know the tubs with the little knobs on the bottom that cost, like, $3,000? Those knobs are bogus. I don't trust those things, even if it comes out to a dollar a knob. I wouldn't go in there without a shower mat. Or a helmet. Or a spotter.

Now let's move on to something even more serious.

Baths.

I love them.

Just one little problem.

Getting into the tub.

At my age, I'm not equipped to lift my leg high enough to get over the lip of the tub. I have to crawl over, like I'm going over the Berlin Wall. You have to raise your leg, vault and roll, and then grab for something to hang on to or pull yourself up and over with, like the shower curtain. This is very hazardous. You could easily pull down the curtain rod and go down with it. The bath is great once you're in it. It's getting in that's the problem. And, yes, getting out, because you encounter the same hazards, only in reverse.

Help is on the way, though.

I was watching a golf match on the Golf Channel with my buddy RJ, and a commercial came on for a new kind of bathtub. The tub's spokesperson, a guy about my age, wearing a puka-shell necklace and a Hawaiian shirt, started pitching this tub, telling me how great it was. Something about this guy seemed familiar. I scooted to the edge of the couch to get a better look. Did I mention that at fifty your vision *and* your hearing start to go? Anyway, I got closer to the TV and ratcheted up the sound. I suddenly recognized the guy because of his voice.

Unmistakable.

Pat Boone.

Yes. Pat *Boone.*

If you said, "I remember Pat Boone," instead of, "Who the hell is Pat Boone?" then this tub is for you.

In the 1950s and 1960s, Pat Boone was a huge recording star, known for singing covers of R & B songs like

"Ain't That a Shame" by Fats Domino and for being un-believably white. I'm not lying. He was famous for wearing shoes called "white bucks." That sounds way racist to me. I think he hung with Anita Bryant and that crowd, too. But now what pissed me off was that he had to be at least eighty-five and he looked my age.

At least my career hadn't spiraled down to the point that I was doing commercials on the Golf Channel for bathtubs.

What am I talking about? If I'm eighty-five and I look as good as Pat Boone—hell, if I'm upright—I'd kill to land a gig selling bathtubs on the Golf Channel.

It took me a few seconds to get past Pat and his puka shells, but I finally focused on the bathtub he was demonstrating.

This was no regular old bathtub. This tub was special.

This tub had a door.

It opened like a car.

You swung the door open, walked in, closed the door behind you, and sat down for your bath. No vaulting, crawling, rolling, or pulling the shower curtain down on your head. Right away this reduced your chances of cracking your head open and drowning in six inches of water.

The tub was deluxe. It came with climate controls, Jacuzzi vents, every tub accessory you could ever want. This was a dream tub. You turned the water on and lay back as the water splashed up, over, and all around you. Your whole body pulsated with pleasure. You could adjust the intensity and temperature to your heart's content. And the best part? When you were finished, you just reached over, shut the water off, stood up, opened the door, and stepped out.

Brilliant.

I wanted one of those. I wanted one bad.

"Look at that tub," my friend RJ said. "You have to be an idiot to waste money on one of those."

"Seriously," I said.

"People are so gullible. They'll buy anything. A tub like that? You gotta be seventy years old and an invalid, or live in an old-age home, or walk with one of those canes with suction cups on the bottom that stick to the floor."

"Seventy? Really? I don't know; you could be maybe sixty-five or even fifty—"

"And who was that old-guy pitchman?" RJ asked. "His face looked like a prune."

"No idea."

"You have to be a pussy to take a bath, anyway."

"I know, right?"

"Or older than crap."

"Baths? Ha-ha-*ha*! *Baths*."

"I'm gonna get another beer; you want one?"

"Nah, I'm good. Thanks. I already had two."

"You're not going anywhere. Have another one. You're such a lightweight."

"Lightweight? Me? Right. Ha!"

RJ left the room. I waited until I heard him banging

around the kitchen before I furiously copied down the phone number that crawled along the bottom of the screen across Pat Boone's Hawaiian shirt, while good old Pat repeated it three times slowly for those of us who are older than crap.

# SAFE SOX

# SPEAKING of golf . . .

Late one afternoon, a week after I turned fifty, I walked the back nine on a golf course near my house. The course was empty, so I took my time, strolling leisurely until it started to get dark. This is one of my favorite times of day on a golf course. I love late afternoon, when the shadows get long and the light turns a soft shade of purple, and I love early morning, when the air is cool and crisp and smells of freshly cut grass.

That afternoon I walked alone down the fairway, stopping occasionally to hit a few shots. I didn't keep score. I rarely do. I'm not interested in the number. How I play is much more important to me than how I score.

As shadows spread over the fairway and darkened the rim of a peanut-shaped sand trap, for some reason I saw a vision of myself as a ten-year-old boy. Me and golf. We go way back together. More than forty years. And whenever I imagine myself as a kid, I'm not playing baseball or the guitar or riding a pony; I'm holding a golf club and smiling.

I taught myself how to play. I'd always loved watching

golf on TV, especially the majors—the Masters, the U.S. Open, the PGA, and my favorite, the British Open, now called the Open. During commercials, I'd grab this old rusted golf club my grandmother kept around the house and I'd go into the backyard. I'm not sure how we ended up with a golf club. I think it was in case we heard a noise.

We didn't have any golf balls, but we had the next-best thing: a lemon tree. I figured lemons are sort of round—well, oval, but in the round family—and even though a lemon doesn't have dimples like a golf ball, it has a rough surface. I thought it was a pretty good substitute. Hey, I was ten. At least I knew that a grapefruit probably wouldn't work.

I pulled a bunch of lemons off the tree and placed them on the ground. I stepped up to each one and, copying the form I'd seen my favorite golfers use, in particular Lee Trevino, I got into my stance and swung at the lemons, cranking it up with all I had, trying to hit those lemons over the backyard fence.

I learned pretty quickly that lemons are not at all like golf balls.

If you hit a lemon on the button, it squirts. Guess you'd call that the sweet spot. Sometimes—rarely—I'd get some lift, and a lemon would fly over the fence and fall into our neighbor's yard. I knew I hit a good shot if I bounced a lemon off my neighbor's dog. The dog would howl and then charge up to the fence and bark at the top of his lungs like Cujo, angry as hell. It was great, because my grandmother would start yelling at the neighbor, "Tell your dog to shut up! I need my rest!"

Most of the time, though, I'd whack a lemon, slice it open, and lemon juice would just squirt out. I guess that's where the expression "turning lemons into lemonade" comes from—a ten-year-old Mexican-American kid hitting lemons with a rusty old golf club in the backyard. I'll tell you this: When I got older and started playing golf for real with actual golf balls, shooting at pins and greens instead of at my neighbor's yard, I discovered that a golf ball was a lot easier to hit than a squishy lemon.

That afternoon, as I walked up the eighteenth fairway, I started thinking about my life and turning fifty and about all the things I wanted to do before I died. I'd accomplished a lot in my fifty years. I'd spent an evening at the White House, dining with the president of the United States. I'd become friends with some of my idols from show business and sports. I'd succeeded in my chosen career, achieved a little fame and a fair amount of money, which I've happily shared with others and unhappily with my ex-wife. I'd survived a serious health scare and set up a foundation to help fight kidney disease. I felt blessed. I'd been granted almost all my wishes. I once read about a guy who asked a wise man, "What do you do when your dreams come true?" The wise man said, "Keep dreaming."

I paused near the lip of the eighteenth green and a crazy thought came into my head, something I wanted to do more than anything else. A personal quest. I decided that I would play every one of the top hundred golf courses in the world.

You have to consider any list with a hundred items on

it a huge challenge. Especially for me, because it involved literally traveling the world. I love to travel, but I was a late starter. When I was a kid, my grandparents never took me anywhere. We hardly left the house. Well, that's not fair. I did go to a few places. I went to:

The front yard.

The backyard.

School.

Kmart.

The liquor store.

I might've missed a couple places. Let me think. Well, Jack in the Box, but that doesn't count, because we didn't get out of the car.

No. We did not go places. We didn't go to the beach. We didn't go to the movies. We didn't go to restaurants.

So I dreamed. I dreamed I went to Disneyland and Dodger Stadium and the Forum. I imagined myself at magnificent white beaches in Hawaii and striding down the windswept fairways of historic golf courses in Scotland.

Now, here comes the weird part.

I didn't picture my face in those places.

I pictured my feet.

Yes, my feet.

Especially as I got older and I imagined myself stepping onto those famous golf courses, I saw my *feet* stepping down onto the first tee at Augusta National. I watched my *feet* walking down the fairways at Pebble Beach and Spyglass Hill, the waves of the Pacific crashing below. I said to myself, "One day, my feet are gonna be there."

Feet. Feet matter. Feet are significant.

Think about it.

When you play golf, hitting a good shot depends on how you move your hips, how you shift your weight, and—very important—where you place your feet. Your stance. You have to adjust the position of your feet every time you hit a different club.

Your feet are your foundation. Your anchors. Your feet ground you. Literally. It's not just me; I'm not the only one who feels this way about feet. Feet are part of our culture.

What do you find in the cement in front of the famous Grauman's Chinese Theatre in Hollywood, or in the sidewalks throughout Hollywood?

Footprints of the rich and famous.

Yes. Their *feet*.

And what about law enforcement? What is one of the main elements of solving a crime? When cops want to track a killer at a crime scene, what do CSI guys look for?

Footprints.

They don't dust for elbows. Or shoulders. Or necks. They dust for fingerprints . . . and they look for *footprints*. A cop doesn't say, "We caught a break. The guy leaned on this door. We got a perfect impression of his ginglymus joint. Let's bring him in."

No. It's all about feet.

I discovered something else that has to do with feet. A life changer, at least for me.

For a couple of years now, I've been doing reflexology. This stuff's amazing. Actually blows my mind. Here's how it works.

I take off my shoes, lie down, close my eyes, breathe, and this very talented woman, call her Lorraine . . . *rubs my feet.*

You wouldn't believe it. It's a miracle. I'm a new man.

Let's just say that I've experienced some stress in my life. At times I have been slightly unpleasant, impatient, irritable, and, I'll admit, a borderline jerk. Okay, I'll be honest: I've been a raging asshole. Also, like a lot of people who grew up on fast food, Slim Jims, beef jerky, soda, and lard, when I stress out, the stress goes right to my stomach. Reflexology has changed all that. I'm a million percent calmer. I've cut way down on my stress. I get no more stabbing pain in the pit of my stomach. I have more energy, better digestion, and a lot more patience. And I hardly ever get sick, because Lorraine, using reflexology, has removed all of my toxins. She also kick-started my qi—my invisible life force, also called my energy field—and got that humming along like a well-oiled machine. I have no idea how she got all this to happen, but she did it. . . .

By rubbing my *feet.*

I was skeptical, too. Mainly because I didn't learn about reflexology from a doctor or a shrink or a medical Web site. I heard about it from a total stranger at the Coffee Bean.

It's not as crazy as it sounds. Well, okay, it's a little bit crazy. I was hanging out at my local Coffee Bean one day sipping some Earl Grey tea, and I started talking to this woman sitting next to me. We started a casual conversation, but before I knew it, we got into one of those deep, intense discussions that I always seem to have with total strangers. I don't know what it is. I can sometimes be more intimate with a stranger at a coffee shop than with somebody I've known for years. For some reason, after I turned fifty, I've become more open and less judgmental. I just let it fly. Got nothing to lose, I guess. Or maybe I'm making up for all the times in my twenties and thirties when I clammed up and brooded, playing the part of the sullen, moody Mexican comic. The truth is, that's not me.

So back at the Coffee Bean, this woman and I started this great conversation over my tea and her Mocha Ice Blended, skipping all the small talk, going right into a heavy discussion about fate and spirituality and alternative medicine. I not only believe all of that; I'm really cool with it. When death stared me in the face in my mid-forties, I became open to almost anything. So when this woman asked me, "You ever try reflexology?" I didn't flinch.

I'd never heard of it, and maybe I did a joke about it or told her I was particular about who touched my feet, but the truth is, I was intrigued. She insisted I try it. She was so convincing and so sure it would work for me that she gifted me an introductory visit with Lorraine. Lorraine came over a few days later. I didn't know what to expect. I admit I was little nervous. I didn't have to worry. She put me right at ease. There was something about her. This quiet, soft energy popped off her. This might sound crazy, but she kind of . . . glowed. I not only liked her; I trusted her. I kicked off my shoes, lay down, and let her have at it.

Within a few seconds, as she was rubbing away, she frowned and said, "Wow. Your kidneys. I'm feeling something. Definitely. A weakness. You have digestive issues. Oh, and here. Base of your colon. Something is definitely blocked."

The moment she said the word "kidneys," I was hooked.

She's been rubbing my feet ever since.

I've now become supersensitive about my feet. And very protective. I don't wear shoes around the house—I go barefoot or wear socks, always have—and this can cause a problem. I have hardwood floors, which I keep clean and polished, but this makes the floor as slippery and treacherous as a hockey rink. What I really needed were socks with traction. I pictured something with tread on the bottom, a combination of a sock and a tire.

I remembered hearing about something called slipper socks. I looked them up online. I found some called Totes, which are basically socks with rubber soles. I scrolled through all the styles. I'm not putting them down, but they weren't my style. They were too . . . girly. I couldn't see myself wearing them. I guess I could walk around the house in them if I were alone. But I'd never wear them if there was anyone else with me. I'd look like a thirteen-year-old girl on a sleepover.

Then Lorraine told me about compression socks. She described these tight-fitting, sheer stockings that go up to your knee or thigh and are great for your circulation. Then, to close the deal, she said, "These are the most comfortable socks you will ever wear."

I got excited. I did a quick search online and found an entire selection of these amazing socks. Well, first I found compression *stockings,* which looked like panty hose my grandmother used to wear beneath her capri pants. Or the kind of stockings a bank robber wears over his face. I stared at them in horror. I saw myself pulling these panty hose all the way up my leg, and my face morphed from my own and became an old Mexican aunt's face, and I started to scream.

*Nooooo!*

I clicked off that page and went to the one with the compression socks.

Better.

Sort of.

First of all, nobody under fifty wears compression socks. It's not a youthful look. Or a stylish look. The guys from *Jersey Shore* do not wear compression socks. Apparently, they don't wear condoms, either.

Compression socks increase the blood flow through your legs. They're for people with varicose veins and poor circulation. In other words, old people. But here's the thing . . . a confession about my compression socks.

I don't care how they look; compression socks are the single most comfortable item of clothing I've ever worn. Ever. It's as if these socks pull everything together in a heavenly way. The first time I slipped on my compression socks, I said, "Whoa. This is all right. This is better than all right. This is fantastic. I love my compression socks."

My only problem with wearing compression socks is that I don't want anybody to know that I wear compression socks. Because even though you can get them online, until you figure out your proper fit, you really need to get them at a medical supply store.

And since I'm trying to maintain a somewhat youthful image, if somebody sees me walking into a medical supply store, I'm dead. Popping into one of those places, you realize that there is a huge old-people industry.

They have a whole section of clothes that are flame-retardant so that we don't set ourselves on fire. There's a wide selection of handrails. By the way, if you need some kind of marker to let you know when you've turned the corner from middle-aged to old, here it is:

When you have to put in a handrail to walk upstairs to bed.

And it's five steps.

You also find many choices of wheelchairs in the medical supply store, some with *ejector seats.*

This is perfect for when you discover that you can't get out of your chair on your own, when you hit, say, fifty-two or fifty-three. All you do is press a button in the arm and the seat flies up and boots you out—ejects you—just like you're in one of James Bond's cars. Except you're not. You're in a damn *wheelchair.*

Then they have special devices that make putting your clothes on easier. I found this tool called a "buttonhook/zipper pull" that has a wire on it that you slip through the buttonhole of your shirt and then you pull it so you don't have to fumble with the button to open your shirt. You just hook the thing through and pull. Works with a zipper, too.

I guess you put it through the other way and the thing buttons your shirt.

Actually, this doesn't sound so bad.

As long as I don't forget where I put it . . .

The bottom line is, this place is for old people. If you want to appear young, you cannot get caught going into a medical supply store. It's worse than if you get caught going into an Asian massage parlor. It's tricky to pull this off, because sneaking into a medical supply store is only half the battle. You also have to sneak *out*.

You can usually control going in. That part's not bad. You just have to look around, make sure the coast is clear, flip your collar up, pull your ball cap down, and run like hell. But coming out? That's the problem. You have no control. You don't know what's going on out there. You have no idea who might be outside walking by, lurking, getting ready to bust you.

"George? Is that you? Yes, it is. George Lopez. How about that?"

"Yes. Hi, there. Hello. What a surprise. I haven't seen you in a while. You're looking great, yes, very trim and fit."

"Did you just come out of that medical supply store?"

"Me? No."

"It looked like you did."

"Oh, see, I came *through* the medical supply store. I was en route."

"En route? From where?"

"The Asian massage parlor. I'm very tight. Muscles bulging. Need to loosen up—"

"What's in that bag? Oh, wow. I don't believe this. Compression socks."

"They're for my aunt. She has bad circulation. And later on she's gonna hold up a bank. By the way, you look like hell."

As long as we're on the subject of feet and my cozy compression socks, I have another confession. This one's even weirder.

As we've established, when you turn fifty, everything starts to go. I've already admitted that I dye my hair. But white hair does not stay confined to the hair on your head. For example, my nose hairs are turning white. I trim them every day. And when I see a white hair popping out of my nose like a little snowy weed, I go right after it.

A lot of times I'll notice a new one when I'm driving. I'll catch sight of it in the rearview mirror. *Pop.* The little sucker will just appear. It drives me crazy, because the older you get, the stronger your nose hairs become. I'm not sure why. There must be some scientific reason. But once a nose hair grows long enough for you to see it sticking out like a little white tail, you know it will be a bitch to pull out. One good yank will not do it. It often takes several. And even one nose hair pull will make you cry.

To yank those things out, you really need a tool. Some kind of implement. A nose hair extractor. I should invent something like that. How great would this be? You insert a tiny button into your fingertip—have it embedded in there like one of those electronic chips you put under your dog's skin so you can track him if he wanders off—then you hit the button and a tiny nose hair extractor shoots out. Flies right out of your finger so you can remove those nasty little nose hairs on the go. That would be amazing. I'm gonna patent that.

By the way, it's not just my nose hairs that are turning white.

My pubes, too.

Sprouting white as Santa's beard. Like a snow bush. I dye that area, too. I cannot allow people to see me—even in the privacy of my bedroom—and say, "Who are you? You're not George Lopez. George Lopez does not have long white sinewy nose hairs and a snowy white pubic area. No. That's not George Lopez. Or if it is, I have to say, what happened to you?"

Now back to the confession. And this has nothing at all to do with vanity.

I paint my toenails.

And I'm proud of it.

At the moment—I'm looking at them right now—I have painted my toenails black. And they are looking *sharrrp*.

Yes, black. Well, a shade of black. I would call this a deep midnight black, not a subtle, soft black that you could pass off as a navy blue or charcoal gray. I am aware of all of the various shades. There are dozens.

Why do I paint my toenails?

Two reasons.

First, as I mentioned, my feet are important to me. You get old, your toes get beat up, your nails get chipped and cracked and ugly and messed up. So I paint my toenails to protect them.

Second, my toes look awesome painted.

Hey, a lot of guys do it.

At least, a lot of guys I know.

The first guy who told me he painted his toenails was Shaquille O'Neal. Yes, *that* Shaquille O'Neal. All seven feet, three hundred fifty pounds of him. I thought, "If Shaq paints his toenails, not only is there nothing wrong with painting your toenails; painting your toenails is cool." So, yes, if Shaq paints his toenails, I'm gonna paint mine. And if you have a problem with that, I'm gonna tell Shaq that you think he's a pussy because he paints his toenails.

I don't paint them myself. That would be weird. I go to a nail salon. Same place Shaq goes to.

First time I went there, I figured I'd just get a pedicure. I wanted to go slow, take it a step at a time. I didn't think about putting on any polish. When the pedicure lady finished, she said, "You want color?"

I said, "No. No color."

She shrugged and said, "Shaquille O'Neal, he come, he put color. He put black."

I said, "Shaq put on black?"

"Yes. Mr. Shaquille put on black."

"You know what? Do that. Give me the same thing Shaq gets. Put black."

"Once you go black, you never go back. Hahahaha!"

She went to work. She took her time, applied the black toenail polish like an artist with a tiny brush. When she was finished, I stared at my feet for about thirty seconds. I felt strange. It felt as if I were looking at somebody else's feet. I wiggled my toes just to be sure.

"You like?"

"You know what?" I said. "It's all right."

That was fourteen years ago. I've been painting my toenails ever since. And I've branched out from black. I've experimented with silver and purple and even veered off a single color and tried designs. I've gone with sparkles and swirls and some spots and crackles. After all my experimentation, I always end up going back to a solid color. Those other toenail designs are too feminine. Painting my toenails seems totally natural now. I can't imagine my piggies without polish. I've become a toenail-painting fool.

I know. It seems crazy. You never would've thought that I, George Lopez, would paint my toenails and actually like the way my feet look. I never would've thought that, either.

When you turn fifty, you shouldn't be afraid to try new things. It's time to expand your thinking. Shake things up.

Some advice.

Before you go into the box, think outside the box.

# SPOONING
# WITH ROVER

WHEN you turn fifty, people assume that you can't possibly date a younger woman. White hair, young woman? No. Doesn't fit. People don't get it. And they can be so rude. I have a friend, a young actress—call her Lindsey—whom I've been mentoring. I've been giving her advice, trying to guide her in business and in life. Lindsey is young, very attractive, and tiny. If you saw me walking down the street with her and you allowed your mind to go to that "is he dating her?" place, you'd think I was dating a toddler. That's how young she looks. But most people refuse to go there. They just *assume*.

**THE POSSIBILITY THAT I COULD BE ROMANTICALLY INVOLVED WITH A WOMAN THAT YOUNG AND THAT ATTRACTIVE BLOWS THEIR MINDS.**

"Oh, hello. Is this your daughter?"

The possibility that I could be romantically involved with a woman that young and that attractive blows their minds. And they don't even give me a chance to introduce her or engage them in conversation. I would prefer this:

"Oh, hello. How are you? Sharon, this is Lindsey."

"Nice to meet you, Lindsey. And how do you know George?"

That's better than people making a huge leap. Then either Lindsey or I have the opportunity to respond appropriately: "We've been friends forever," or, "We're dating," or, "We met five minutes ago at Cheetah's. She gave me a lap dance." I hate people getting up in my face and rudely asking, "Is this your daughter?"

We've become a country of know-it-alls. I think it's because of all of the information instantly available to us with the tap of a finger. If I'm sitting in a restaurant with a friend trying to enjoy a nice quiet lunch, people have no problem snapping a picture of me with their smartphones. That drives me crazy. I will never turn away a request for a picture or an autograph if somebody asks me. But people who sneak pictures of me without asking and then post them on the Internet piss me off.

And it makes it so much harder to lie.

"Where are you, George?"

"At the car wash. Then I'm gonna go pick up the dry cleaning and maybe hit a bucket of balls—"

"Really? I just saw on Twitter that you're at Cheetah's, sitting in the front row. 'Hey, guess who's in the next booth? Hashtag Georgelopez.'"

Social media, man. Suddenly everyone's a reporter.

It really messes you up.

Even if you are a gifted liar, born with a poker face, like me.

ONCE I stopped lying, everything changed.

Including my relationships with women.

When I was younger, I never did well with women. I don't know what it was. Maybe it was because I used to be incredibly shy and insecure. Even so, I wasn't terrible-looking, and I always tried to dress nice. It didn't matter. I could not get a date. Not one. Zero. Women just didn't find me attractive. I couldn't get laid at a women's prison.

I tried. I went out with friends, went to bars, clubs, concerts. I looked for women. I was on the prowl. But nothing ever happened.

One time, in the eighties, I went to a bar with some friends. We found a table, ordered drinks, and started pounding them back. The room got hot and smoky and I started to feel sweaty and a little buzzed. The air smelled of sex. People looking for it. People willing to give it up. The deejay cranked the music so loud you could feel the bass vibrating in your gut. My friends all got up and moved toward the dance floor. Each one found a partner and paired off. I sat alone at our table, watching everybody else, nursing a beer, feeling empty.

I scanned the room. That was when I saw her, sitting by herself, a few tables away—a woman about my age. A vision. The kind of vision you see lurking around a corner in one of the *Alien* movies. To put it kindly, this woman was very unattractive. Of course, she had other qualities. She was also fat.

Perfect.

I was sick of getting shot down. I was done with good-looking women checking me out, sticking their noses up, and turning away. I had set the bar too high. In order to get into the game, I needed to lower my standards. If you swing for the fences on every pitch, you'll only strike out. You have to start by hitting singles. Just get on base. Then you can slide into home.

I polished off my beer, stood up, and strolled coolly over to her table.

"Hello," I said.

I gave her my best, widest smile.

She swiveled her head in my direction. Close up, she actually looked scarier than she did from across the dark bar. Her lips parted to reveal fangs. I jumped back.

"Hi, there. So, yes, I was wondering," I said. My voice cracked and then squeaked. "Can I buy you a drink?"

She plopped a meaty arm over the back of the chair next to her. She ran her eyes up and down me slowly, as if she were scanning me at airport security. She parted her lips again and her fangs appeared in full and rested on her lip. I think I saw smoke coming out of her nose.

"No, thanks," she said.

I blinked. I coughed. I swallowed.

"Excuse me?" I said. "I didn't hear what you said. Loud in here."

"I'm good," she said. "I'm waiting for my friends."

She grunted and swiveled her scaly head away.

"Oh, okay, fine, great, I'll just, you know . . . I'm a little surprised, but, yes, cool, not a problem, very nice meeting you; enjoy molting—"

I slunk back toward my table, looking for a way to disappear, hoping that a hole would suddenly open in the floor so I could dive in and flee. As I groped for my table like a blind man, I thought, "Unbelievable. *She* turned me down? Mothra said no? How can that be? I know how: I'm a loser. No. That's not true. I'm the biggest loser in this bar. It's official. I'm the worst dude in the room."

When I look back at that night and think about the lull in my dating life, that short twenty- to thirty-year period, I see another guy. I was a different person. I lacked confidence. I somehow felt *less* than everybody else. And I was so shy that I scared women off. My grandmother always used to tell me, "Shies don't get shit." She was right, but at that time knowing I was shy made me feel even shier. That's the main reason I couldn't get a date. Women wanted no part of me. I turned them off. I'm talking about *all* women, even those who were so desperate that they would date anyone who walked upright and didn't drool. Except me.

Everything changed when I turned fifty. I experienced an attitude shift—very simple and basic. Since I had arrived at an age that was closer to death than not, I decided first to chill, to slow down, to take it easy, and not to get agitated over little, insignificant things. Second, I decided to live my life my way, to follow my instincts and not be so eager to do what other people said.

I applied all of this to my relationships with women. I

refused to become one of those sad fifty-year-old dudes you see sitting alone at the end of the bar. You know who I mean. There's always one pathetic old dude nursing a drink, playing with his cocktail napkin, looking lost. For one thing, you should never go to a bar alone at fifty. You need to travel with a pack of dudes, no matter what your age. And it's important to monitor how you look. Dudes in their fifties walk a tightrope, style-wise. You put on the wrong clothes and you fall right off. You've seen these guys. They're trying to look young, or hip, or at least relevant. They sit at the bar wearing mom jeans and a sport jacket with patches and maybe a scarf. Besides the sad doe-eyed look that creeps across their Botoxed faces, their drink is the giveaway. It's always an old guy's drink, a Manhattan or a highball or some cocktail the twenty-five-year-old bartender doesn't even know how to make. The world is zipping by and this poor guy is standing still. You see him fingering his iPhone, trying to figure out how to send an Instagram. Not his fault. Technology comes at you in a blink. There's always something new you have to learn, and our fifty-year-old brains don't move as fast as they used to. Ten years ago he would've been able to handle Instagram, no problem. Now he's sitting in a bar and he's clueless, holding the thing upside down and sideways, shaking it, trying to get it to work.

When you turn fifty, you have to learn to accept the natural flow of life. You must accept who you are.

And, brothers, you have to accept your penis.

If you live long enough to get to the point that your penis doesn't work, so be it. Allow it to stay flaccid, in honor of its previous service. You should not force it to stand at attention. Let's celebrate this honorable member. It's fine. And don't worry about taking the little blue pill. Women understand. If a woman would refuse a fake Louis Vuitton purse, she should refuse a fake erection.

## BROTHERS, YOU HAVE TO ACCEPT YOUR PENIS.

A lot of dudes use enhancement—call it Hamburger Helper, well, Hot Dog Helper, I guess—and they don't tell their wives. The wife thinks, "Oh, my God, he's as vibrant at fifty-four as he was at twenty-four. Of course, he always seems to need an hour notice."

Just accept it. Be man enough to say to your wife, "My penis worked for forty years; we had some great times; we traveled; we made love all over the world. So let's shake hands, get the same haircut, and move on."

I'm into younger women. It has nothing to do with their supple, hard bodies. Well . . .

They're more open to new things. They're not set as cement in their ways. Older women come with too much baggage. In the relationship with my current girlfriend, I think it's so much better that I'm the one with the baggage. I don't have a big enough place for two people's baggage.

At this point, the relationship with my girlfriend is pretty new. I have yet to experience that feeling of dread that comes over you when you wake up in the morning, turn over, see this person sound asleep next to you, and say to yourself, "Look at her. So beautiful, so peaceful. I wish she would leave."

I've not felt that way. Not yet.

We're pretty compatible. She's young, likes to stay up late and sleep in. I'm old; I like to get up early and play golf. This is ideal. Although like most women, she hates golf.

I can't figure out why that is.

I just know that when a woman sees her husband or boyfriend heading out the door with his clubs, she says, "You're not playing golf, are you?"

"Well, yes, I am."

"Again?"

"I play every Sunday; you know that—"

"Fine. Go. Have fun. *Enjoy.*"

I don't get it. What did we do? We're going to a golf course, not to a strip club.

For some crazy reason women feel threatened by golf. It's almost as if golf is another woman. Or worse: They think our relationship to golf matters more than our relationship with them. Or maybe it's this simple: Women see that we have a good time playing golf, which means we're not having a good time with them. They can't stand the thought that we might actually have some fun without them. Maybe if we lied.

"George, where are you going? You look miserable."

"I feel miserable. I have to play *golf.*"

"Again?"

"I know, right? What a pain in the ass. If I didn't have

to do this, I wouldn't. You know that. I'd much rather have brunch with you and then go shopping for shoes."

In every relationship I've been in, when it comes to golf, there's always that terrible moment of truth. You have to brace yourself for this question: "What do you guys talk about out there on that golf course for five hours?"

I don't want to lie. I want to tell the truth. I want to say, "Well, pussy, mainly."

But that would only fuel their hatred of golf. In some cases, God forbid, it might motivate them to take up the sport so that they could *play with us*. When my ex-wife threatened to take up golf, I told a friend that I would cut off my arms so I wouldn't have to play.

The truth is, we don't really talk about pussy that much. When we play golf, we talk about . . .

Let me think.

Actually, we don't talk. We really don't. That's another reason we don't want to play with women: We don't want to talk when we play golf. We don't want to talk at all. We just want to play. In silence. Without thinking about what to say, or what we think, or worst of all, what we *feel*. The hell with that. This is the hardest thing for women to understand. When I go out with three guys to play golf, not only don't we talk very much; ninety percent of the time we're not even together. We're off on our own, hitting our shots, alone, by ourselves, not thinking about anything but golf. My definition of bliss.

Even my young, understanding, very compatible girlfriend can't stand that I play golf. Usually I sneak out of the house when she's still asleep. By the time I get back, she's just getting up and we're ready to begin our day. But one morning, I took a shower, slipped into my golf clothes, and slowly, quietly, on tiptoes, started to head out the door. I heard her rustling in bed. I turned back and saw her sitting up, her eyes wide-open.

"Hey," I whispered. "I'm going out."

She took a moment to look me over. Finally, it registered that I had on my golf clothes. She blew out a funnel of air that hit me like a tornado and roared like an oncoming train, *"Nooo!"*

My head snapped back from the force of her scream. "I'm just . . . playing golf. . . . I'll be back in a few hours—"

*"Nooooo!"*

I can't think of one thing that would cause me to freak out the way my girlfriend does over my playing golf. Oh, I've had reasons to go nuts. But I've been cool. I've held back. Call it my new after-fifty attitude. For argument's sake, here's a reason that might've have caused other people concern. Put up a red flag, so to speak.

One night when we were out—after we'd been dating awhile and things started heating up—she said that if our relationship was to go any further, I would have to share her affections. She reached into her purse and an adorable Chihuahua puppy poked her head out. My girlfriend nuzzled the dog. The dog squealed and barked happily and licked her face. I had to admit the dog was pretty damn cute. My girlfriend lifted the dog all the way out. The dog had on a pink dress.

"I hope the dog's a girl," I said.

"Of course. Well? What do you think?"

"Cute," I said.

"Hold her."

"No, that's okay—"

She pressed the dog into my arms. The puppy squirmed for a couple of seconds, then snuggled against my chest, got comfortable, and looked up at me with big round adoring eyes. I caressed her little head gently, and then, I swear, the dog smiled.

"Hold up. Did she just smile at me?"

"Yes! That's the test. You passed. She likes you." Then she smiled, not so much out of happiness but from relief. "Our little family. This is going to work."

I like dogs. I've had dogs my whole life, starting when I was a kid. They mostly stayed outside, because my grandmother said she was allergic. I guess that's possible, although I don't ever remember her sneezing. Whenever I sneezed she told me to cut it out; I was still going to school. In order to skip school, I'd better be bleeding, which, by the way, she said she could make happen.

I think she just didn't want to deal with the dogs inside. Today she couldn't use that dumb allergy excuse, because people breed hypoallergenic dogs. They also combine breeds on purpose. I used to have a dog that was half spaniel, half poodle. We called it a mutt. Today there are no more mutts. That breed is now a very special and desirable breed known as a spanieldoodle. My dog was the result of two dogs that did it in the neighborhood.

Today a poodle gets knocked up by a Labrador, you call it a Labradoodle, and it costs you $5,000 for a puppy.

People plan the mating of their dogs as if they were arranging a canine couples' retreat. They get the dogs together and let them romp and frolic and fool around like they're on some doggy getaway weekend in Maui. When I was a kid, you didn't plan anything. Your dog got out and came back pregnant. I'd say, "Hey, the dog got knocked up." Then, when the dog gave birth to this spanieldoodle, I'd think, "I don't want this. My dog got laid by a cocker spaniel. It's ugly." Not only does that ugly mutt now cost five grand; it's considered beautiful.

Dogs used to be just dogs. Modern dogs have become privileged, even elitist. I've seen dogs look at me like they're better than I am. You can see it in their eyes. They look down on you.

I once got involved with a woman who really loved her dog, a huge German shepherd named Hans, who I swear didn't like Mexicans. Shortly after she moved in, I got a bad feeling about Hans and their relationship, which should have been a red flag about her as well. Right away I got the sense that Hans didn't like me. There was something about the way he looked at me. He would sniff in my direction, turn his nose up, and make a face like I smelled. He would sort of frown, as if he accused me of farting. Usually you blame the dog. This dog blamed me.

I mentioned this to my new girlfriend. I told her I thought her dog was jealous of me. She laughed it off. "You have a great imagination," she said.

"I do," I said, "but I'm not imagining this. I'm telling you the dog doesn't like me. I know I'm right about this."

I was so right that one night I came into the bedroom and found the German shepherd lying in bed spooning with my girlfriend. They were both sound asleep, snoring loud enough to wake the neighbors.

I froze in the doorway. "What the hell . . . ?"

The dog lifted his head, glared at me, gave me a disgusted look that said, "Oh, it's you," then dropped his head onto the pillow and went back to sleep.

Now, I know some people like to spoon with their dogs, but this didn't sit well with me. I realize people are just being affectionate with their dogs, sharing a moment, and it's no big deal. It's not like that woman I read about a while ago who used to drink wine and watch TV in bed with her pet orangutan. Every night she'd pour herself and her orangutan a couple of glasses of a good cabernet, drop a sedative into his glass, and they'd snuggle and watch a movie, something they both could relate to, like *Rise of the Planet of the Apes*. One night, she decided to change things up and poured the orangutan a pinot noir instead. He got pissed and tore her face off.

I don't want to say, "Lady, hello, what did you expect?" but *what did you expect?* I'm not putting a panther or a chimp in my bed, even if I gave him a bottle of Scotch and a couple of Vicodin while we watched HBO. I know where to draw the line. Spooning is far enough.

I didn't think I'd have to worry about any weird behavior with my new twenty-something girlfriend and her Chihuahua puppy. This dog was into me, and the three of us liked to hang out. I did have to adjust to one minor quirk that kind of threw me off.

My girlfriend liked to dress the puppy up in dresses, skirts, and other girly doggy outfits. Come on; it's not that bad. Actually, dressing the dog up didn't really bother me. I kind of got into it. One day I put a Lakers jersey on the dog—same one I had on, only smaller—and the two of us settled onto the couch to watch the game. I even let the dog sip my beer.

Then a few months later, tragedy struck.

The puppy got sick and died. Just like that. The poor little dog contracted some rare illness and that was the end. Doggy heaven. Unbelievably shocking.

My girlfriend fell into a terrible depression. The loss of her little puppy knocked the wind out of her. She couldn't get out of bed. She just lay there, day after day, comatose, sobbing, not eating.

I was determined to do something to snap her out of her funk. I tried cheering her up with jokes, inviting her friends to visit, spending as much time with her as she wanted, giving her as much space as she needed. I even tried *listening*. Hard as hell for guys to do, but I did it. I didn't interrupt or nod off or reach for the remote. Not once. Nothing helped. I was at a loss. Then my friend RJ told me about a pet psychic.

"You won't believe this woman," RJ said. "She converses with the dead."

"By converses, you mean . . . You don't mean . . . What do you mean?"

"She talks to people's dead pets."

"Okay, see, right there, I'm suspicious, because dogs can't talk," I said.

"True, but they have thoughts. Supposedly. This pet psychic reads their thoughts."

"I see. She reads their dead thoughts," I said. "They can't be the dog's current thoughts, because the dog is currently dead."

"I don't know how it works."

"So, after a dog dies, the thoughts live on? Is that it? Where do they go? Do they get captured in a thought bubble? Or maybe dogs continue to have thoughts even after they die. Maybe their body passes on but their mind keeps going. Is that how this works? Help me out here."

"How should I know? I'm just saying that maybe if your girlfriend talks to her dog, she'll feel better. Knowing the dog's in a better place and all."

"Okay, I see, yes, well, this sounds insane. Off-the-charts nuts. Where is this pet psychic freak weirdo, anyway?"

"Hermosa Beach. You have to pay cash. Plus I heard she's not cheap."

"I bet. She probably charges an arm and a paw."

A pet psychic. I couldn't believe I was even having this conversation. Like I was ever gonna drive halfway to San Diego down the horrendous 405, the world's busiest, most congested, most migraine-inducing freeway, and pay through the nose—er, snout—cash, so my girlfriend could talk to her dead dog.

I told my girlfriend about the pet psychic, laughing pretty much the whole time, maybe being a little bit dismissive. I noticed as I was talking that her eyes got wide. When I was finished, she sat up in bed. It was the first sign of life I'd seen from her in a week.

"We have to go," she said.

"To the pet psychic? See, I'm not sure she's legit; plus we have to go on the freeway—"

She slid back down into the bed and gave me what I can only call a sad, puppy-dog look. Melted me. That sealed it. I had no choice. I made an appointment with the pet psychic.

And that's how we ended up stuck on the 405 in rush-hour traffic at noon, which is not even rush hour, but on the 405 you're always stuck in rush-hour traffic.

I was intrigued. I actually wanted to meet the pet psychic. I've always been fascinated by death. I don't know why. It might sound morbid, but I've always wondered what it's like to be dead. I know, of course, that you stop breathing and people can't see you anymore and you can finally quit worrying about paying your car payment and your credit card minimum and your cable bill, but what does being dead feel like? As we motored down the 405 freeway doing a brisk three miles an hour, I realized I had a lot of questions for my girlfriend's dead dog.

Mainly, though, I wanted to find out the answer to the big question:

What really happens when you die?

Well, to start with, I think the body is a container for the spirit.

In fact, I've heard people say that you choose your body. That may be so, but as you get older, your body falls apart, and I don't think you choose that. Maybe you just choose your body in the beginning. How does that work? Does your spirit go to a showroom and pick out the body it wants? Is it like a dealership? Can you haggle?

"This body is short and dumpy, and I can see the hair is already thinning. I can tell that you're rolling back the hair. You're not fooling me with that comb-over. This body is going bald at thirty. How much for something taller and better-looking, with a thick head of hair?"

I know that whatever body you choose, it will deteriorate. And when your body goes, it does not go quietly. You will leave a little something behind—some farts, some pee, possibly a tiny bit of shit. That's why some genius invented Serenity protective undergarments.

So, yes, I had a lot of questions for the pet psychic.

I had never been to a pet psychic before—never heard of a pet psychic before—but I do believe in psychics. I think that some people have a gift: the ability to see into the future, even, in some cases, to connect with people who have passed on. You have to be careful, though. Not everybody who says they're a psychic is the real deal. I wouldn't stop on the way to the airport to get my fortune told by some psychic sitting outside her house in a folding chair. But if I got a solid recommendation from someone I trust, then I would see that psychic. I actually had an unbelievable experience with a psychic once, in the eighties. Totally freaked me out. And got me into a ton of trouble.

This psychic, I'll call him Bandini, was really different. He was a hyphenate: He was both a psychic and a comedian. I know that sounds like a joke, but it's not. He would perform his stand-up in clubs or at people's homes, and after he finished his set, he would do readings. I went to see his show with a woman I was dating pretty seriously. After his set, I wanted to go to my place and have sex, but she wanted to stay and have her palm read. As far as negotiating our plans for the rest of the evening, we were very far apart. But I told her to go for it. I wanted to make a call anyway.

While my girlfriend was having her reading, I found a pay phone—this was before cell phones—and called this *other* girl I'd been seeing. Casually. Once in a while. Couple of times. We'd gone to high school together and lost touch. Then somehow we reconnected and had gone out the week before. Casually. Couple of times. To a motel.

"How did it go?" I said to my girlfriend in the car after her reading, not really caring that much how it went. I cared mainly about getting her back to my place.

"Interesting," my girlfriend said. "He read my palm."

"That's kind of a cliché, isn't it? Not very original."

"Call it what you want. He definitely saw certain things."

"Really? Like what?"

I should say that at this point, I thought all psychics were full of crap, able to wow you by telling you a few "amazing" things that they figured out just by being observant.

"Well," my girlfriend said, clearing her throat, sounding a little annoyed, "Bandini looked at my palm for a long time. Then he frowned and said, 'I see that you're with somebody. The guy you came here with? Is he your boyfriend?' I told him yes. You are my boyfriend, right?"

"Yes," I said. "Of course I am. Sure. Why are you asking me?"

"Because Bandini said you're seeing someone else."

I nearly drove off the road. "That's crazy," I said. "The guy's nuts."

"He saw a 'J.' Very clearly. He thought her name began with a 'J.'"

"A 'J'?" I started coughing. "Ha! See? Right there. That's wrong. I don't know anybody whose name starts with a 'J.'"

"Well, he wasn't sure about the 'J' being the first letter of her name."

"That's because Bandini the psychic comedian is full of it."

"He may have been confused."

"May have been? He was definitely confused. He was confused because he's full of *shit*." I gripped the steering wheel to keep my hands from shaking.

"No, he was confused because he kept seeing the word 'windjammer' along with the letter 'J.' He also saw last Tuesday and Thursday nights really clearly, like in a vibrating purple color."

My cough rose up from my chest and clutched my throat. I couldn't breathe. I thought I would pass out.

"You okay? That's a nasty cough."

"I'm good. I had a couple of tacos while you were with

the psychic. I think the meat was tainted. The sauce was a weird color, too—"

"It's not true, is it?"

"No. Of course not. Not at all. Not a word of it."

Bandini nailed it.

All of it.

I saw my old high school flame Tuesday and Thursday night at the Windjammer Motel in a sleazy room with purple carpeting, purple walls, and a purple bedspread.

Oh, and her name?

Janine.

**WE** arrived five minutes early for our appointment at the pet psychic. I parked in front of the pet psychic's house, a small, boxy one-level Spanish on a nondescript street close to the beach. I noticed that the street was a dead end, which, when you think about it, seemed appropriate. We looked at each other, hesitated, then got out of the car. Instantly, all feelings of nervousness or weirdness fell away. A sense of relaxation washed over me. I reached for my girlfriend's hand. We walked up to the pet psychic's door and knocked.

After what felt like at least five minutes, the door opened and a seventy-year-old woman pulling an oxygen tank appeared. She looked like an older version of Meryl Streep. Swimming pool blue eyes. A full mane of reddish hair. A warm smile bordered by two deep dimples. She put her hands together in prayer, and sort of bowed.

"Welcome," she said. "I'm so happy to meet you."

And then, without thinking, I instinctively hugged her. I reached out and put my arms around her. I have no idea why. I just felt compelled to hug this Meryl Streep–look-alike pet psychic. I didn't want to squeeze too hard, because she felt fragile, and her breathing was labored and came in short spurts, wheezes, but as I hugged her I felt a warm sensation go through me, like an electrical current. I'd never seen this woman before in my life, and yet I was enjoying one of the great hugs of all time.

"Yes," she said. "I know."

She slowly pulled away from me and put her arms around my girlfriend. They hugged even longer, and my girlfriend started to tear up. The pet psychic patted my girlfriend's hair gently and whispered something, and my girlfriend nodded. The pet psychic closed her eyes and spoke quietly in her raspy voice. "We have a lot to talk about," she said.

She gently broke the hug and started walking toward a room in the back of her small house, dragging her portable oxygen tank behind her like a tail. We followed her past a cluttered living room completely filled with crystals—crystals on an old television set, a credenza, end tables, shelves. In the center of the room, on a coffee table, a gold Buddha sat surrounded by even more crystals. As we walked behind the pet psychic, wind chimes sang outside a large picture window and cast a golden light across our path.

We came to a back room, a kind of porch, and the pet psychic gestured toward a love seat facing an overstuffed armchair. We sat down and the pet psychic sat heavily into the chair, arranging her oxygen next to her. She smiled at us, and then she closed her eyes. She sighed, let out a long, cleansing breath, and fell into a deep trance.

After a full two minutes, she said, "Yes. Uh-huh. I see a strange-looking dog. A spaniel crossed with a poodle, maybe. A mutt."

My girlfriend looked at me in confusion, but I nearly fell off the love seat. "That's my dog! From when I was a kid. I had that dog for sixteen years."

The pet psychic dropped her head and covered her face with her hands. "This dog liked to go in the car."

Wow. How could she know *that?* Lady, every dog likes to go in the car. This pet psychic was a fake. The oxygen tank was probably a prop, a way to tug at your sympathy and get you to cough up more money.

"This dog would go crazy whenever you grabbed your keys," the pet psychic said. "That was his signal. You would grab your keys and he'd think he was going in the car with you."

Whoa. She hit that on the head. I swallowed. "Yes," I said. "It was kind of funny."

"When this dog got old, he developed problems with his hips. Terrible. Finally, you had to put him down."

Damn. Two for two.

"Yes," I said softly. "That's true."

"You brought him to the vet and you left. You knew it was the end, but you didn't stay with him. You couldn't face it. You knew if you stayed, you'd lose it, that you'd fall to pieces. You tried to pretend that you were tough, that it didn't matter. But it did matter. You left because you knew that was the only way you could hold it together. You didn't want to cry."

I bit my lip. I could feel the tears welling up.

"He wants you to know that it's all right. He understood. He knew how you felt. He knew you loved him."

"I didn't know what to do . . ." I said, the tears trickling down my cheeks.

"Are you crying?" my girlfriend said.

"No," I blubbered. "Allergies."

"He forgives you," the pet psychic said. "Now, he says, you have to forgive yourself."

I lost it. I tried to fight back my tears. And failed.

"He was a good dog," I said.

The pet psychic pulled a tissue from a box on the table next to the love seat and handed it to me. I dabbed my eyes and blew my nose. My girlfriend shook her head and rested her hand on my forearm.

"Now you," the pet psychic said to my girlfriend.

The psychic closed her eyes and drifted off into that trance again, this time for a solid three minutes. When she opened her eyes and spoke, her voice seemed higher and had lost its raspy sound.

"I hear her," she said.

My girlfriend gripped my hand so tightly I thought she would snap off a finger. The pet psychic nodded and spoke in an even higher voice. "'Hey, dying was as much of a shock to me as it was to you,'" the pet psychic said.

My girlfriend gasped.

"'It was quick,'" the pet psychic said in that new voice.

"'I wanted it to be quick, because I knew you couldn't handle a long illness. Believe me, I didn't want to go through that, either.'"

The pet psychic scrunched her forehead; then she coughed and her raspy voice came back again. She opened her eyes and scanned our faces. She stared into my girlfriend's eyes. "It was a freak thing, wasn't it? Unexpected. The dog was so young. A puppy."

My mouth dropped open like a trapdoor. I thought, "How does she know this? Puppies don't usually die. We never said one word to her."

"Was she in any pain?" my girlfriend asked her.

"No, no, none at all. She just said, 'Shocked me as much as it did you.'"

"But no pain?" my girlfriend said.

"No. But. Oh. Aha." The pet psychic scrunched her forehead again.

"What?" I said.

"I see her again," the pet psychic said. "She said . . . Wait . . . Okay, I got it. . . . She said that she did not like being dressed up."

My girlfriend let out a small scream.

The pet psychic raised her head and looked up into the ceiling. She frowned. "I see clothes. A lot of clothes. Tiny clothes. Piles of tiny clothes. I see a teeny pink dress and pink hat."

"I put that on her for her birthday," my girlfriend said, then turned to me. "She looked adorable, didn't she?"

"Oh, yes. Yes, she did. Absolutely. Very cute."

"I thought she liked that outfit," my girlfriend said.

"Apparently not so much," I said.

"The clothes choked her," the pet psychic said.

My girlfriend grabbed herself around her midsection. She looked stricken. "Is that why she got sick? From the clothes? Tell me it wasn't from the clothes."

"She didn't get sick from the clothes," the pet psychic said. "She just felt uncomfortable. The clothes were too tight."

"That sounds right," I said. "I get very uncomfortable when my pants are too tight. But I can undo them because I have thumbs. I can even take them off. The dog? No."

I shook my head sadly.

"I didn't realize. . . ." My girlfriend's voice trailed off.

"She had a lot of clothes," I said to the pet psychic. "That's true. A lot of tight-fitting clothes."

My girlfriend frowned at me. "Did you ever think her clothes were on too tight? Did she ever look uncomfortable to you?"

I squirmed in my seat. I tried to catch the pet psychic's eye, but she was staring off, avoiding me. I looked back at my girlfriend. "To tell you the truth, a couple of times I thought the dog didn't really dig it when you put clothes on her."

"When?"

"Well, okay, when I put the Lakers jersey on her, she seemed cool, relaxed, comfortable. But when you put on that tight dress, the pink one, or that hoop skirt, or those snug little capri pants, she would just sit there. She never moved. She would not move at all. When you turned away, she gave me a look that said, 'Take this off me.'"

My girlfriend folded her arms. "She did not."

"She did. You could see it in her face. 'I hate this outfit. Take it off me.' You could see it in her eyes."

My girlfriend shot me a look that could kill, then looked past me out the window. "You never said a word."

"I'm telling you now. It's a little late; I grant you that. I was going to say something the next time you put on the tight clothes, but then, you know, she got sick, and then . . ."

The pet psychic slowly swiveled her head and looked into my eyes. She held her gaze on me, gave me a ferocious stare. "She wants to talk to you," she said.

"Me?"

"Yes. She has something important to say."

"Really? I'm surprised. I mean, we liked each other, we got along great, but we weren't close."

My girlfriend elbowed me.

"I'm open. I'll listen. What does she want to tell me?"

"She says . . ."

The pet psychic stopped, then nodded as if she were listening to someone giving her complicated instructions. She began again.

"She says she's sorry that she was such a nuisance when you came home. She wants to apologize for barking so much and for running around and around your feet like a lunatic."

This was uncanny. How could she know that? Every word the pet psychic said was absolutely true.

"That's okay," I said. "Tell her it's okay. I might've jumped or yelled a little bit at the time when she nipped my toes, but I'm over it."

"You yelled at her?" my girlfriend said.

"No. Not at all. Not really. I might've raised my voice a little bit. She was biting my toes. I didn't want her chewing up my nail polish, choking, and dying. I guess it wouldn't have mattered. . . ."

"There's something else." The pet psychic jammed her eyes shut and scowled. "I'm getting something with . . . golf clubs."

I moved forward in my chair. "Golf clubs?"

"Yes. I see a bunch of golf clubs lined up against a wall."

I had to keep myself from leaping out of the chair.

In my house I keep several golf clubs lined up against the wall.

How could she know *that*?

"Well, that's . . . amazing," I said. "You've never been to my house, but you're right: I have a lot of golf clubs lined up against the wall."

I could feel my girlfriend looking at me, but I was too freaked out to look at her. The pet psychic stifled a small chuckle. "Golf, yes, of course. She wanted to go with you."

"With me? To play golf? The dog?"

"Yes."

Talk about irony. My girlfriend hated when I played, but her dog wanted to go with me. The dog loved golf. That little cute, adorable puppy loved *golf.*

"Maybe we should've put golf clothes on her instead

of dresses. Knickers like Payne Stewart. A tiny golf cap. Little cleats . . ."

We both started crying then, my girlfriend's tears flowing as a release, my tears coming from picturing me with the Chihuahua dressed in a tiny golf outfit on the first tee at Pebble Beach. Lee Trevino would've fallen over.

"My baby," my girlfriend said through her tears.

"Fore," I said through mine.

# SEX AT FIFTY OR . . . *FRIGHT NIGHT*

**SEX** after fifty is a whole new ball game.

In many ways, it's better.

When I was younger, I would do anything to get laid.

Actually, that's not true.

I would do anything for the *possibility* that I might get laid.

As soon as Friday came, I would prepare for my night out, and I'd obsess over every detail like I was a general planning a war. I'd think where to meet someone to get laid, who to get laid with, what to wear, what to say, and how to act. Should I try to be cool? Funny? Aloof? Interested? Bored? Should I channel Marlon Brando (ultra cool and tough), Richard Pryor (hilarious and sensitive), or Richard Lewis (neurotic and Jewish)? Hey, I'd do whatever it took.

I paid special attention to my appearance, not the least of my concerns being . . .

How should I smell? Should I go with your basic manly scent and just use Lava? Or should I roll on Axe? Or do women really prefer men who dab on English Leather? What about my hair? Should I go with the wet look, blown dry, or sculpted with product? And how about clothes? Always a challenge. I'd open my closet door, whip through my clothes like a maniac, and start to sweat. So many decisions, so many choices, so much pressure.

In the end, none of my preparation or worrying mattered. As I told you, I wasn't all that successful with women. I'm lying. I went, like, zero for my twenties and two for my thirties.

As I got older, I gained more confidence and I got luckier. Strange how that happens. Ever notice that the more confident you become and the harder you work, the luckier you get?

**ALL THE WOMEN I DATED SEEMED TO SHARE SOMETHING IN COMMON, ONE SPECIFIC QUALITY: THEY WERE ALL CRAZY.**

As I started going out more, I began to notice a pattern. All the women I dated seemed to share something in common, one specific quality.

They were all crazy.

Yes. I was attracted to crazy.

Or crazy was attracted to me.

Every woman I dated was nuts.

And if they weren't nuts, they snored.

I could handle crazy. That was easy. I ran like hell or changed the locks or I moved.

But a woman who snored?

That was impossible. Because snoring sneaks up on you. You don't expect it. It's an ambush in the middle of the night.

The worst was when I began seeing a woman seriously and I asked her to move in. Then—and only then—did she start to snore. What is the deal with that? Where was the snoring before? Was she holding her breath all night for months before she moved in?

When I'm talking about snoring, I don't mean that cute, breathy sexy little humming sound that can be a total turn-on. No. I'm talking about that openmouthed, sour-smelling roar coming out of the face of the person lying next to you that sounds like a garbage truck backing up while grinding its entire load into pulp.

This woman snored louder than a death-metal band. Try to feel sexy with that noise blowing out of the person who's unconscious beneath your sheets two inches away.

The first time I heard her snore, I woke up like I'd been shocked with electricity. I shot right up into a sitting position. I thought the television had exploded. Then I realized that the horrifying sound giving me an instant migraine was actually my recent live in girlfriend deep asleep, snoring like a jet engine coming in for a landing. I couldn't sleep in the same bed with her. I couldn't sleep in the same room with her. Hell, I couldn't sleep on the same *floor* with her. I had to sleep downstairs. That's how loudly and violently she snored. And the moment her snoring went into high gear, my sex drive went into park. Doctors have a name for this condition now: sleep apnea. They suggest going to sleep with a Hannibal Lecter mask over your face. Nothing kills your sex drive faster than sleeping in the same bed as a serial-killer cannibal.

After I turned fifty, my feelings about sex changed.

I was no longer obsessed with getting laid. I started seeing the whole person and not just her body. I wanted to really get to know someone. I wanted to allow a relationship to build. I felt the need to take my time, to relax, to laugh, to connect. As I changed my attitude toward sex, the sex actually got better, and I became a better partner. I think a lot of guys would benefit from changing their approach to sex. How did I do it? Easy. I just related sex to football. Starting with . . .

If you're on offense, you shouldn't always throw the bomb on first down.

You've got to set things up. Try a couple of running plays, mix in a slant, a screen pass, a draw play up the middle. Then go for the end zone. Don't shoot for pay dirt right away. Don't get sucked in. *Come on; go deep.* No. What if you throw an incomplete pass? Or worse, what if you throw an interception? You do not want that.

Worst of all, if you score too early, you're gonna end up fumbling.

Bottom line: Sex after fifty requires a different approach. You have to adjust. Some adjustments occur automatically.

First, the room is darker.

Almost pitch-black.

The darker, the better. I used to like lava lamps and incense. Now I like blackout curtains. My partner may want to see my naked body, but I've already seen it, every day, four, five times a day, and trust me, it's better to keep her in the dark. When I was younger, I could have all the lights on and the windows open and sunlight streaming in. We could do it with a mirror on the ceiling or illuminated by a spotlight or under lights as bright as a night game. I didn't care. And it didn't matter when—night, noon, dawn, dusk. There was no bad time. It could be anywhere, too. In a car, a swimming pool, a closet. I didn't need any advance notice or warm-up, either. I was always ready.

"What did you say? You want to go now? Great. No, that was plenty of warning. More than enough. Let's get it on."

But when you turn fifty, all that changes. You especially lose spontaneity. That's one of the first things to go. You have to plan ahead. You need plenty of notice so you can put the booty call on your schedule. You have to tap the ass-tap time right into your smartphone calendar.

"Honey, how's Wednesday night?"

"Wednesday night? Let me see. Well, I have a thing, but it's not important. I can move it. And that other thing can wait. Okay, yes, Wednesday night will work. Thursday night would be better. And actually, Friday's even better. That gives me plenty of time to plan and get ready."

Yes, sex becomes something you plan. An event. An activity. Hopefully a regular activity. Many therapists and experts on aging suggest that sex is better after fifty if you remove the guesswork. They say you should make a night out of it, preferably the same night every week. Sunday night you have dinner with the in-laws; Tuesday night you bowl; Wednesday night you bang. Once a week seems about right. More than that can put strain on your heart. Less than that can cause you to dry up. A weekly booty call gives a guy enough time to gear up, to get his head into the game. Wednesday is perfect. It's hump day, right?

A lot of guys count it down.

"Five more days to go. Four more. Three. Two. Today? Is it Wednesday already? Sex day is today. Wow."

This may sound like I'm lying, or that the world has turned upside down, but when some guys turn fifty, they don't always look forward to the scheduled weekly sex date. As the night gets closer, a feeling of dread hits them. It could be performance anxiety, or feeling the loss of spontaneity, or hating that sex has become an obligation. Or maybe they're just not in the mood. That over-fifty drop in testosterone can do that. Whatever the cause, when we know that the night has come and calculate what is expected of us, there can be pushback. We don't want to be told what to do. We're men. We're in charge. We're supposed to be the ones who do the deciding. Yes, sure, that's a lie. We never had control of sex. But now, after fifty, we start to get resentful. We start thinking of excuses, especially if there's something good on TV, like a game or a wildlife special or a reality show about bounty hunters or restoring a World War I helmet.

Some guys try to get out of it. They hope for a tapeworm or some kind of virus. Some guys throw themselves down the stairs. That usually works. Others feign migraines. Or, better, stomach pains. No woman wants to be with somebody who's got diarrhea. That's your real out.

The truth is, it's really about respect. And appreciation. And commitment. I want to be there for my weekly Wednesday-night party. If you're in a relationship with a truly caring woman, just being together affectionately, lovingly, intimately, can be all she wants. Of course, if it leads to something else . . .

I wasn't always this way. I admit that there were times, especially in my marriage, that I may have been a tad selfish.

One warm Saturday afternoon in late May 1997—that day still sticks in my head—I promised my wife that I would go with her to a strawberry festival. Now, I like strawberries as much as anyone—nothing wrong with popping a few strawbs into your mouth for a snack, or spreading some strawberry jam on your toast—but a strawberry *festival?* An entire weekend devoted to strawberries? With games and rides and people walking around dressed up like actual strawberries? Really? Why did I agree to this? What was I thinking? But I'd made a commitment. I promised I'd go.

Until I found out that Tiger Woods had entered the Byron Nelson Tournament and was playing in a twosome with a friend of mine. Tiger had just won the Masters and was on a roll. I knew he would kick my friend's ass, but I wanted to see my friend go head-to-head with Tiger. How many times do you get to watch your buddy play with Tiger Woods on national television? I wanted to get comfortable on my couch, pour myself a couple of adult beverages, roll out some snacks, and watch the golf tournament on my big screen.

I broke the news to my wife. I told her I changed my mind. I was gonna stay home and watch golf. I wasn't leaving the house.

"What about the strawberry festival?"

"Unfortunately, I have a conflict. Something came up. Something unforeseen and unavoidable. I have to watch the golf tournament."

"But you said—"

"I know what I said. And I meant it. At the time. But my friend's playing against Tiger. Could be a once-in-a-lifetime thing. I can't miss that. You can go to the strawberry festival without me. You'll have a better time. I don't love strawberry cream pie all that much, especially in the heat."

"I'm not going without you."

"Well, you're gonna have to."

Things escalated from there. Kind of got heated. Shouting, screaming, finger-pointing, name-calling. I don't remember exactly what we said, but I remember doors slamming and a lot of crying. My wife got upset, too.

Bottom line: I got my way. My wife went off to the strawberry festival, and I settled in to watch the golf tournament. I found my spot on the couch, kicked off my shoes, aimed the remote and—

*Fffzzzt.*

The cable went out.

One minute I'm looking at Tiger; a second later I'm staring at a pitch-black screen.

"Son of a bitch." I whacked the back of the remote with my palm. That usually works. I tried the TV again.

Nothing.

I couldn't believe it.

"The damn cable's *out?*"

*Whack, whack, whack.*

Nothing.

Then I realized what happened. "She probably cut the wire."

I groaned miserably. I figured this was either an example of my luck or God getting back at me for bailing on my wife.

I never did see Tiger and my friend playing in the Byron Nelson, but at least I avoided the long lines in the heat at the strawberry festival.

But to this day—sixteen years later—I gag whenever anybody mentions anything to do with strawberries.

"Interested in dessert?"

"Tempt me. What do you have?"

"Pies. We bake all our pies here. We have apple pie, cherry pie, and our house favorite, creamy, gooey strawberry cream pie—"

I gag, cover my mouth, and bolt into the bathroom.

# HAVING KIDS AFTER FIFTY OR . . . ARE YOU CRAZY?

I'VE been blessed to have accomplished a few things in my life, but when people ask me, "What's your number one achievement?" I always say, "That's easy. My incredible daughter, Mayan."

She's the best thing that ever happened to me. Everything else is in second place.

And believe me, I'm glad I became a father in my thirties, because when you're over fifty, having a kid will age you rapidly.

That's the last thing you need—something that makes you older faster.

If you're over fifty and you get into a serious relationship with a younger woman, the question of having kids will come up. It's inevitable. And you won't like it. One night you'll be in bed minding your own business, watching TV or sorting through your golf tees, and your girlfriend, wearing something slinky and sexy, will cuddle up next to you and very casually start having "the conversation." It usually begins with her gently touching her finger to your lip or nibbling on your ear, and then she'll say something like, "I was just thinking about how wonderful you are and how lucky I am. . . ."

Uh-oh.

Get ready.

Here it comes.

Pretty soon you'll hear something like, "I was wondering . . ." and then you'll zone out. Most of what she says after that will buzz right by you, but a few key phrases will stick, like, "My biological clock is ticking," and, "Such gorgeous kids together," and, "I'll do all the heavy lifting," and the absolute worst, "You'll make an amazing daddy."

While she's making her pitch, you'll be having a conversation with yourself. You'll be thinking, "Do I want a kid after fifty?" and phrases will start flying around in your head, like, "Having a heart attack playing catch," "Say good-bye to nooners," "A half a million bucks for private school, cash, before taxes, *cash*," and, the killer, "I'll be *seventy-five* when the kid graduates college; I hope I recognize her."

I knew a guy in his fifties, Marco, whose twenty-something wife, Terri, snuggled up to him one night and started having the "the kid conversation." Marco already had grown kids. Terri purred and cooed and nibbled and Marco felt his pulse race, but not because of the purring and cooing and nibbling. He was starting to freak out about having another kid.

"Listen, I love you," Marco said to Terri. "I want to be with you, but I've already had kids. I really don't want to have a baby."

"You won't have to do anything except get me pregnant," Terri said. "That's it. That's all I ask. Get me pregnant and you're done."

That didn't sound so bad to Marco.

"That's it?" Marco said. "Hit it and run?"

"That's it," Terri said.

"Well, I'd be willing to do a bare minimum. You know, like make a cameo appearance in a movie."

"Okay, how's this? I want to be completely honest and realistic. What if I set a limit for how much time you have to spend with her and I absolutely stick to it? How about you agree to be with her for two hours a day?"

Marco mulled this over. "Two hours a day? And I'm done?"

"I promise. After two hours, you hand the baby over to me, and you're done until the next day."

"I'm gonna hold you to that," Marco said.

And he did.

His daughter is four years old now.

"I spend two hours a day with her and then my daughter and Terri know that Daddy's tired," Marco told me. "I come home. I roll around with the kid. We spend a quality couple of hours and then I hand her over to Terri."

This arrangement sounded crazy to me. I didn't get it. It sounded both too radical and too good to be true, at least for someone over fifty who didn't want another kid.

"Run this by me one more time," I said to Marco. "You just hand the kid over? How does that work?"

"Easy. I say, 'Here, Ter, take her.' Most of the time I stick around, but sometimes, if I want some peace and quiet, I go to the condo."

"I thought you got rid of the condo when you got married. You said it was too small."

"No. I kept the condo. It's way too small for me, Terri, and the baby. But it's perfect for me alone."

I've heard of separate bedrooms, or a man cave in the basement or out in the garage, but Marco arranged to have separate *houses*. Or in his case, a house and a condo.

"This is kind of like *Mad Men*," I said. "You got the big house in the suburbs and the apartment in the city."

"Yeah. A crash pad."

"I have to admit," I said, "it sounds pretty good."

"Oh, no," Marco said. "It's great."

This would never work for me. I couldn't have two totally separate places to live. And I could never have a kid at my age. I'm too old, too vain, too set in my ways, and did I mention too *old*? I don't want my kid to look at me and say, "Grandpa." Kids can see the difference between young and old. They can pick out an old person. You're right in front of him. Normally a kid's field of vision fills up with young faces—his friends, his parents, his teachers, his friends' parents. My kid would see all that and one old, wrinkled face. Mine.

No.

I don't want that.

And I don't want his friends to say, "I really enjoyed playing with Grandpa George. He's cool, for an old person. He played with us for almost five minutes before he started breathing heavy and holding his side."

No. I'm not gonna do that.

I've done the math. If I have a kid when I'm fifty-three, by the time the kid graduates high school, I'll be seventy-one.

*Seventy-one?*

I can't make that guarantee. I may not live that long.

You know when somebody says, "Hey, it has a lifetime guarantee"? That doesn't mean anything anymore. It used to be a big deal. If you bought a coffeemaker and it came with a lifetime guarantee and then it broke, you could take it back and the store would give you a new one.

I can't offer my kid anything close to that. For all I know, my lifetime guarantee means four months.

And when you have a kid, time speeds up. You age faster.

One day I was having a drink with some guys after a round of golf, and this one guy pulled out a picture of his family—him, his wife, and his two little kids. The guy was beaming, happy as hell. He couldn't wait to show us this picture.

Here's what I saw:

Two cute little kids, an attractive young woman in her late twenties or early thirties, and this decrepit old dude who looked like the picture of Dorian Gray. His skin was pasty and wrinkled, his hair was thin and sparse and looked glued to his bald head, and his earlobes hung down to his shoulders. They looked like mud flaps. He seemed so out of place with this vibrant, young family. He didn't fit.

The picture gave me the creeps.

I don't want people taking that picture of me. And if I did have that picture in my wallet because my wife forced me to carry it around, I sure as hell wouldn't show it to anybody. Or I'd Photoshop George Clooney's head over mine.

I can't see myself doing even the most basic things, like getting the kid dressed. I throw my back out putting on my own socks. I pull a muscle sleeping. What's gonna happen when I try to pull on the kid's pants or tie his shoes or get him into a shirt? I'll be at the chiropractor for weeks.

And then to get the kid to do anything, you gotta raise your voice sometimes. You know there's gonna be yelling and push back. Then the kid will cry and you'll have to yell louder. Hey, I'm already old. Sounds bother me. Recently, I went to see the band Rush in concert at the Nokia Theatre in L.A. The guys are friends of mine, so I hung out with them in their dressing room before the show. As they were about to go on, Alex Lifeson said to me, "Hey, man, you want earplugs?" I laughed and said, "Really? Do I look that old? No, thank you." So, I listened to them play bareback, sans earplugs. My ears rang for a week. It felt like somebody whacked me on the head with a crowbar. I learned some valuable advice that night:

If it's too loud, you're too old.

So, clearly, I've become sensitive to certain sounds.

Like a kid crying. I can see myself out at the park or at a game and people start to yell at me because I'm yelling at the kid and the kid's crying, and then somebody says, "Hey, can you shut that kid up?" I hate when a dog barks next door. How will I deal with a kid crying nonstop in my own house?

Having a kid will make you older instantly. It will not be a slow build. It will happen, bam, just like that, like a bullet to the head. You'd better psych yourself up, because as soon as the kid's old enough to walk and move on his own, you're gonna be dragging your ass to all these stupid kid places. These are places designed for kids and parents who are much younger than you and in much better shape. I'm talking about places such as Gymboree, and Karate Kids, and those insane birthday parties at Chuck E. Cheese's. That place is a nightmare. My head is pounding just thinking about all those screaming kids in there. And without a doubt, you'll be the oldest person in there. People will come up to you and say, "Excuse me, are you the owner?"

Now, take a moment and think about the *parents* of these kids. Yes. Your kid's friends' *parents*. Again, do the math. Let's say you're fifty-eight and you have a five-year-old kid. Look around Chuck E. Cheese and check out the parents. They're all twenty-seven. You know how old you are? You could be *their* parents. Some dude is dragging his kid around Chuck E. Cheese's and you could be his father. But, no, you have to worry about his kid shoving your kid's face into a pizza. It's wrong and it's a complete pain in the ass.

To me, this whole having a kid after you turn fifty is like a wrestling match.

You're in the ring with your opponent. You're grabbing, you're grappling, and you quickly start to lose your leverage. Your opponent squirms out of your grasp, gains the advantage, and gets into position above you. That's it. You're done. The end. Because once you lose your leverage, you are at the mercy of the person who's on top. And you know what's on top?

Age.

All I can hear is that big clock ticking.

*Tick, tick, tick.*

Every day is another tick.

The clock is running out, dude.

You can do your best. You can chase after your kid in the park until your breath gives out and you're sucking wind and your side starts to stab with pain and feels as if it's about to split open. You can scream at your kid to stop shoving pencils up his nose until all you hear is the sound of your own voice screaming and you think your head is going to explode. You can try to deal with all the best intentions but you can't avoid this—

*Tick, tick, tick.*

Yes, when you have a kid after fifty, life is a wrestling match.

And you're about to get pinned.

# KEEP FIT OR DIE TRYING

IT'S important to stay fit at any age, but you really have to watch yourself after fifty. Once you hit that number, you start to go downhill fast. Let's be honest: Our bodies are not built to last. And after fifty? Damn. When I wake up and peruse my body, I'm always amazed at what I see.

"Who the hell is that? Is that really me? Is that what I look like? What the hell happened? Where did that twenty-year-old go? Who is that old guy staring back at me?"

The first thing I do every morning is check myself in the mirror. I want to see how much I've aged in the middle of the night. I can tell by looking at my hair. If it looks better than it looked when I went to bed, fuller than I remember, then I know I've held off the downhill slide a little bit longer and it's gonna be a good day. Then, feeling as if I dodged a bullet, I take my first shower of the day.

**WHEN I WAKE UP AND PERUSE MY BODY, I'M ALWAYS AMAZED AT WHAT I SEE.**

By the way, you may have thought that the first thing I do every morning is take a piss, but I've already been up four times in the middle of the night. And, trust me, those four trips to the bathroom have not been any picnic.

Let me start by saying that I love pajamas. I collect them. Pajama bottoms, to be exact. I have accumulated twenty or thirty really nice pajama bottoms in all different patterns and colors—red, white, and blue; dark green; purple; purple and gray; stripes; solids; flannels; all kinds—because when I was a kid, I never slept in pajamas. We couldn't afford them. In the winter I slept in my jeans, and in the summer I slept in my underwear. I didn't like sleeping in my jeans, because my legs would sweat no matter the temperature and I would stick to the denim. It would be like sleeping in a thick, heavy, stiff sack. But I *hated* sleeping in my underwear. I was a restless sleeper, and I would toss and turn and get all tangled up. I'd wake up with both my legs jammed into one leg hole. Felt unbelievably weird and uncomfortable. I also looked like a bell with my legs sticking out together as the clapper. I vowed that if I ever made any money, I'd buy myself really comfortable pajamas.

Here's how much I love pajamas:

I want to be buried in them.

Why not?

People say death is like sleeping, right? That doesn't sound bad. I love to sleep. And if I'm gonna be sleeping for all eternity, I'm wearing pajamas. I think funeral directors agree with me, because they always put a pillow in the casket. So forget the stiff black suit that they put on the stiff. And the uncomfortable dress shoes. I want to wear my pajamas and my slippers.

I'm so happy that I wear pajamas to bed that I resent getting up in the middle of the night to go to the bathroom. I just want to stay snug under the covers. I've actually considered keeping one of those little bottles that the hospital puts right by the side of the bed, just in case. Then when I got the urge in the middle of the night, all I would have to do is roll over.

In the meantime, I hit the head the way most normal men over the age of fifty do—every couple of hours, like clockwork. I always keep an extra pair of pajama bottoms handy, though, just in case during one of my bathroom runs I accidentally dribble a little pee onto my pajama bottoms. It can happen. In that case, I swap out my old pajamas and pull on the spare pair. No big deal. I've learned to do this in the blink of an eye. It's like changing the tires at NASCAR, except I'm a pit crew of one.

I've also learned to let your dreams be your cue. Doing this can save a two a.m. pajama-bottom swap-out. If you find yourself suddenly lost in a lovely dream in which you're wading in a beautiful warm stream, so warm and soothing that you can actually *feel* the water, force yourself to wake up, because you're about to ruin that really expensive pair of flannel pajamas that you bought at Barneys. Yes, that stream is about to overflow into your pants. I guess that's why they call these the golden years. I used to think the name came from Greek mythology and the ages of man. No. It doesn't. These are the golden years because there's a real good chance you'll be peeing in your pants.

So, back to the morning routine. You've peed,

checked yourself in the mirror, and it's time to step into the shower. I find that first shower exhilarating. I take my time, scrub myself, and enjoy the heat of the wet bristles of water softly pummeling my body. Now, a very important pointer:

Everybody should have a robe. Doesn't matter how old or young you are, you need a robe. If you're young, then you can pretend you're hiding something wonderful. A surprise. A gift. Even if you know what the gift is, it's always better to wrap it up. Much more exciting that way.

If you're over fifty, don't worry about giving anybody a gift. I've come to terms with the fact that I'm now at the age when I look better clothed than naked. So, definitely, keep your body wrapped up. And keep a robe close. You don't want to have to walk across a room to get to your robe. You do not want to take the chance that you will see yourself naked. In fact, stay in the shower long enough for every mirror in the bathroom to steam up so you don't accidentally catch a peek at yourself. This advice is worth repeating:

Keep a robe close.

I keep my robe right outside the shower. All I do is reach out and grab it. No strain, no fumbling. I even double-check that my robe is in go position the night before. I take no chances.

Sometimes when I scrub myself with soap, I close my eyes and I think, "Why did I close my eyes? I don't have any soap in my eyes." Then I remember: I don't want to see myself. That's why I closed my eyes—to protect myself. Listen, this is a fact: Guys chase boobs their whole lives. If you live long enough, you'll get the ones you've always wanted. Except they're on you. I know guys who say, "I don't like big boobs. I like them smaller, just about a handful." Well, wait around. You'll get 'em.

Keeping yourself in shape is really important, but you have to be careful what activities you do, what sports you play, what type of exercise you choose. When you're in your twenties, you feel invincible. You never get hurt unless you actually do something to get yourself hurt, because in your mind, you're still in high school. You play soccer, or hockey, or basketball, or hardball. Some guys even drag their wives or girlfriends along to watch them. Believe me, they don't want to be there, and when you're married for a few more years, they will make you pay.

When guys hit their thirties, they keep playing the same sports that they should've given up ten years earlier, but now their bodies have started to let them down. A lot of dudes keep playing basketball through their thirties and into their forties. They're playing with fire. All of a sudden—*rrriip*—all these guys tear their Achilles, which is God's way of telling you to sit the hell down and choose another activity. Golf. Or pool. Or craps.

When you pass fifty, you hurt yourself without doing anything. You pull muscles and tear tendons while you sleep. I woke up one morning, and I couldn't move. I blamed the mattress. It had to be the mattress, because I honestly didn't do anything. All I did was sleep. The only thing I could come up with was that the mattress messed me up. I couldn't accept that maybe I pulled a muscle changing position on my pillow.

A couple of months ago, I decided that I had to do something to get in better shape. I play golf, I stretch, and I'm pretty flexible, but I needed to add some aerobic exercise to build up my wind and strengthen my heart. Plus I was worried about the bad genes in my family. My grandmother had heart issues in her forties. I realize that part of her problem was both cultural and the time we lived in. In her experience, nobody joined a gym and nobody cared what they ate. My grandmother lived on a diet of lard, butter, pork, beans, and cheese. Salad? There were no salads. Nobody had heard of a salad. It was like an exotic food, or something you could get only in a French restaurant.

My grandmother tried to be weight conscious, but she didn't work out or walk or run or do any form of exercise. I remember one day, when I was around eleven, she came home with a box. She carried this thing into the house and set it up in the middle of the living room. She said, "This is a sweatbox. Very expensive. It's good for you. Don't touch it."

She left the room and I circled the thing like it was some strange, magical creature. I reached out and rubbed the side for one second, then drew my hand back immediately as if I'd been burned. A couple minutes later my grandmother came back in wearing a bathing suit. She had a towel draped around her neck. She opened one of the sides of the box, stepped inside, closed the box around her, hit a switch somewhere, and turned the hot box on. The box hummed. I stood riveted, watching the sweat start to bead up on her forehead. She closed her eyes and patted her forehead with the towel. Then she opened her eyes and saw me staring at her.

"What now? Don't you have something to do? Don't just stand there. Go play. I'm exercising."

I guess my grandmother didn't lose any weight, because when I came home from school about a week later, the sweatbox was gone. But my grandmother didn't give up. She was determined to lose weight. One day I found her rummaging through the kitchen cabinets.

"I gotta lose weight," she mumbled.

"What happened to the hot box?"

"I junked it. No-good piece-of-crap ripoff."

"What are you looking for?"

"Not your problem. Ah. Here it is." She pulled out a large black plastic bag, the kind you fill up with leaves when you rake the lawn. "I'm gonna put on a plastic bag, because I gotta lose some weight. This is gonna work."

She cut a hole at the top of the bag for her head and two holes on the sides for her arms. She wriggled the bag over her head, yanked it down over her body, and lashed the middle with a belt. "What now? What are you looking at?"

"Nothing," I said. I couldn't stop staring at her wearing the Hefty bag.

"Close your mouth. This is not your problem. But if you don't stop staring, it'll be your problem."

I don't remember how long she wore the plastic bag. Felt like a month or more. Every morning she'd slip the thing on while she did all her work around the house— housework, cooking, cleaning—wearing that plastic bag like it was a dress. Whenever she moved, you'd hear this annoying crinkling sound throughout the house—*vwwsh, vwwsh, vwwsh.* Finally, she gave up on the plastic-bag dress and started wearing Saran Wrap under her clothes, which is something personal trainers recommend today when you do crunches or sit-ups, to help you sweat off pounds and tighten your abs. When it came to Saran Wrap around your waist, my grandmother was ahead of her time. But I never saw her do crunches, and I don't think she lost much weight.

I'm not one for joining a gym or fitness center. To me, those places seem like meat markets—nightclubs with less clothes. When you're over fifty, you really don't fit in. You sit on the bench in the locker room. You start to get undressed. You peel off your T-shirt and suddenly you experience the dreaded "one-hair phenomenon." You've got one hair coming out of your arm, one coming out of your wrist, one out of your shoulder, and, worst of all, one long hair popping out next to your nipple. You're not in the best shape anyway, which is what got you there in the first place, so the one-hair phenomenon is about the last thing you need. And then you sneak a glance at the guy getting dressed next to you. He's young, confident, and completely ripped, and you say to yourself, "Why am I here?"

Which is why I started walking the stairs.

I live in a three-level house in the Hollywood Hills—an upstairs with the bedrooms; a downstairs with the living room, dining room, and kitchen; and a lower level with a guesthouse. One day I went down to the guesthouse and I happened to look up at the flight of stairs that led from where I was, the bottom to the top— guesthouse to upstairs—and I estimated that I had at least fifty stairs inside my house. Suddenly I had an epiphany.

I could get in shape right here, in my own house, on my own time, for free. I wouldn't have to go to a gym that was really a meat market. I wouldn't have to hire a trainer who would make me stick Saran Wrap under my shirt while he pinned my legs down as I did crunches. I wouldn't have to stare at a bunch of hard bodies in some workout video engaged in soft porn, pretending they were exercising.

I would simply walk up and down the stairs in my house five times a day. I didn't need a membership or any equipment. All I needed was a pair of decent tennis shoes.

I'd already come to peace with the idea that when you work out after you turn fifty, you're just fixing what's inside. I came to that conclusion several years ago, when I discovered that I could lift weights like a maniac every day for hours and my body would look exactly the same. As soon as I figured that out, I stopped lifting weights. Now the best I can hope for from working out is that my doctor will look at my blood panel and lower my dose of Lipitor. "Oh, my God, look at you. You must be working out. I'm gonna reduce your Norvasc to ten milligrams."

That's your victory. That's your winning the hundred-yard dash, sinking the game-winning three, hitting your walk-off home run. "George, wow, your cholesterol level has dropped to one eighty. Oh, my *gosh*. What have you been doing? I'm so proud of you."

Let's be clear: Stairs are no piece of cake. In fact, after fifty, stairs are a huge, annoying problem. When you're twenty, you don't think twice about climbing stairs. You don't even walk; you run up, taking two stairs at a time. You race your buddies to the top. Now if I go to an important meeting and the elevator's out, I say, "Great, well, I'll just call the dude and tell him I was here but the elevator was out. Sorry."

So I changed into my workout clothes, put on my tennis shoes, laced them up, stretched a little bit, got good and loose, and then I hit the stairs. "Five times," I told myself, "five times is my minimum. I'll do five reps today, then build up. By the end of the week, I'll get to my goal, ten reps, and then I'll see how much more I want to do from there. I know I want to walk the stairs for at least forty-five minutes, then get to an hour."

I started at the top.

Smart.

I inhaled; I exhaled, swung my arms, and walked down the stairs.

That's one rep.

I walked up the stairs.

Two reps.

I walked down the stairs.

Three reps.

I walked up the stairs.

Four reps.

I gasped. I panted. I held on to the wall for support.

Sweat gushed off me, soaked through all my clothes. I felt like I had just stepped out of the shower. I put my hands on my hips and walked in a circle. I took a deep breath, summoned up all my strength, and went back down the stairs.

About halfway, I tasted bacon.

I hadn't eaten bacon in three months.

I slowed way down.

With the bacon taste filling my mouth, I took the stairs one at a time as if I was five years old. Or like I was eighty.

Then a thought shot into my head.

"Why am I doing this? I'm not gonna live long enough to be in great shape."

But I had to get to the bottom.

I looked down. I felt dizzy. My vision blurred. But I was determined to finish. Pressing my hand against the wall, I took another step. And another. And one more.

Almost there.

Just three more stairs.

It's always the last three stairs. Those last three are killers. If they made flights of stairs without those last three, everybody would be happier.

I know this: When I build my own house, I'm gonna design it with three less stairs than everybody else's house.

So, bottom line, after that day, I gave up walking the stairs. No more walking that flight of fifty steps from up-stairs to the guesthouse and back, five times every morning, every day, the way I almost did, well, once.

Instead, I do what I call inadvertent workouts, which I find just as effective and strenuous.

If I'm in the living room and I have to go upstairs to get my wallet, that's one rep.

If I'm upstairs and I want to get my phone charger that I left in the kitchen, that's a half.

Hey, it adds up.

# WARNING: TEXTING MAKES YOU BLIND

THE AARP found me. They sent me a whole packet with a magazine and information about health insurance and other stuff you need to know after you turn fifty, as well as a bunch of wonderful senior-citizen discount coupons. They also included my very own personalized AARP card welcoming me to the club. At first I was pissed, because this packet made my age so *official*. But I quickly accepted it. What am I gonna do? I'm fifty. I'm not gonna lie about it.

This AARP, man, they are on it. They don't go away. They track every old person. They're like bloodhounds. I got my AARP card before I got a birthday card from any of my friends. I don't know how they do it. They must have spies. They must hire people in the neighborhood who work undercover posing as the guy next door. You know who I mean. The guy who's always mowing his lawn or washing his car.

"Hello? AARP hotline? Yeah, listen, my neighbor George Lopez has been acting strange. Lethargic. Despondent. Morose. I found out he's turning fifty in three weeks. Yeah, I'm sure. Get him."

They are so on it. If somebody you know over fifty

disappears, don't call the cops. You're wasting your time. Call the AARP. They'll find him in a minute.

The AARP emphasizes how important it is for people over fifty to take control of their health. It's crucial for us older people to watch what we eat and drink, because our bodies change. We have to monitor what we put into them.

When I was in my twenties, I never thought about what I was gonna eat. My guys and I used to have eating contests. We'd go to Bob's Big Boy and we'd see who could eat the most food. The losers bought the winner's meal. Or *meals*. We'd go to Big Boy because it was close and they served a ton of food.

We'd start with an order of chili and spaghetti, which was a light dish consisting of spaghetti and marinara sauce piled high on a plate topped with a half-pound slab of flame-broiled hamburger and then covered with a glob of chili and cheese, served with a salad. Lose the salad. We substituted fries.

That was the appetizer.

Then we'd all get Super Big Boy Combos, two all-beef patties on a grilled sesame seed bun with lettuce, tomato, American cheese, dressing, and special relish. That was the regular combo. The *super* combo, which is the one we got, added fifty percent more meat and doubled the cheese. This came with a salad, too. Lose the salad. We substituted fries.

Next we got their famous chicken breast sandwich— grilled chicken on a sesame seed bun, Swiss cheese, lettuce, tomato, special sauce, and, yes, a salad—lose the salad; we substituted fries.

If you're weren't full yet, you got another chicken breast sandwich, more fries, and another Big Boy Combo, and then, of course, dessert, usually their "decadent" hot-fudge cake, which was a delicate palate cleanser to end this light meal: scoops of vanilla ice cream sandwiched between two layers of devil's food cake, smothered in a river of hot fudge, and covered with a cloud of whipped cream.

We washed it all down with thick milk shakes.

I never won. I never came close. I barely made it past round one of the chili spaghetti and a few sips of the milk shake. At the end, we'd all chip in and pay the winner's check while he was off in the bushes "digesting" his food.

I can't imagine someone over fifty suggesting an eating contest. I can barely finish the food I order.

"Hey, George, you know what would be great? How about we get a group of guys together, go to Big Boy, and have an eating contest? Gorge ourselves. Get really sick. Like back in the day. Come on; it'll be *fun*."

"Are you crazy? I don't have any Prilosec on me. Hell, there's not enough Prilosec in the world."

I've never been a big eater. As a kid I developed a strong gag reflex. I can tell immediately when something is not fresh. I'm like a food psychic. I think it's from seeing the milk carton change color in our refrigerator. Forget about lettuce changing color, going from green to brown. Yes, I've seen the milk *carton* change color. You knew the milk was bad. You didn't need to smell it. You could see it.

"Grandma, this milk is bad."

"Then don't taste it. Just swallow it. Drink it fast. Close your eyes."

I'm not a big drinker anymore, either. Another sign of age. I've become a lightweight. You drink differently when you're in your twenties. You haven't really lived yet, so you haven't truly experienced sorrow. Life is all fun. You don't have anything to be mad at. You go out with friends, you barhop, you eat, you get drunk, and you're extremely happy. You hug your friends. You laugh. You dance. You kiss everybody. You have a great time. The next morning you wake up and you think, "Wow, what a night. What a great time." You take a shower and you're good as new. Your body recovers quickly, because it's still making melatonin and creating endorphins and firing on all cylinders. You go to work and look forward to the weekend, when you can get drunk and happy all over again.

When you get older and drink, you black out. You wake up with a tremendous headache. It feels like a guy is inside your head blasting through your brain with a jackhammer. You can barely move. Your whole body throbs. Your skin hurts. Your hair hurts. Your eyebrows hurt. The thought of food disgusts you. You swear you'll never drink again. Your blood pressure shoots through the roof because you forgot to take your Norvasc or your beta-blocker or whatever medicine you're on. You sit up and the room spins. You fall back down and slam the pillow over your face. Then you start to remember details from the night before and you get depressed, because you realize you said things you should not have said and you shouted and cried and pocket-dialed somebody and threw up in the corner and now you can't face the day and you are beyond miserable.

Yes, I've been there, and I vowed I would never go back there again. I have to be careful when I drink for all those reasons. Hard liquor puts me in that dark place. Now I nurse maybe one vodka and cranberry juice and call it a night. Anything else is too heavy. I can't do cream drinks. No White Russians or Baileys, nothing like that. Gives me heartburn. Or maybe I'm lactose intolerant. That could be it. Or gluten. It might be gluten. Somebody told me I was allergic to gluten. I know there's gluten in booze, especially in brandy and beer. I'm getting to the point that I don't care anymore.

I know I could handle a couple of beers, but I won't do it. I'm too vain. Beer is way too fattening. I don't want to wake up one morning with a big stomach hanging over my pajama bottoms.

When you turn fifty, you have to change your lifestyle. You don't have a choice. You're no longer a kid and your body can't handle the stuff it once did. I understand that everybody needs an outlet and people want to escape. I get that. But it's too late. You had your fun. I know change is hard, but you have to start taking care of yourself.

If you can't do it on your own, get help. Some cultures like to get everybody involved—family, friends, coworkers, clergy, the entire community. They have what's called an intervention. That's when twenty people rally around a person who has an issue with drugs or alcohol and lovingly confront him.

We're the opposite. In our culture, you couldn't get twenty people to come together *unless* you gave them drugs and alcohol. We don't have interventions. We have parties. We don't want some violent, obnoxious drunk spoiling our party. Other cultures say, "Let him in. We'll intervene, make him confront his addiction. Perhaps we can convince him to seek professional help. Bring him in."

We say, "Get that asshole out. He drinks all our beer. Then he gets loud and obnoxious and picks fights and steals our stuff. I've got my TV in here. He's a whack job. Keep him the hell *out*."

We're not unsympathetic. We just keep them out and hope they get fixed on their own . . . while we party.

I took an interesting path. No intervention, of course. I started drinking way early, and I was the last of my friends to smoke pot. I was only an occasional pot smoker. I never got into other drugs very much—well, okay, except for pills a little bit, because there were so many of them around the house. To be honest, I really like pills. I don't pop them like Pez or anything. In fact, I rarely take a whole pill. I'm fine with a half.

I do have a favorite. Vicodin. Fantastic. My go-to drug. I once said, "I was gonna take yoga, but then I found some Vicodin lying around the house, so I took those."

I take Vicodin to loosen me up and lessen my aches and pains. I like to pop a half in the morning right before my shower so when I get out of the shower, I'm ready to face the day. And if I've taken a Vicodin and I happen to catch a glimpse of myself naked under my robe, it doesn't freak me out so much. Try it. But just a half.

If I am completely honest, I'd admit that I take half a Vicodin once in a while to dull the pain of getting old. Turning fifty is such a jolt to the system that you don't need reminders every minute. But it seems as if there are so many signposts that appear in front of you so often that you can't avoid having a reminder of your age constantly shoved in your face.

One example: the early-bird special.

I used to see a sign outside a restaurant advertising the early-bird special, and I would drive right by without giving it a second thought. Now when I see a sign that says, EARLY-BIRD SPECIAL FROM 4 TO 6 P.M. FRIED CHICKEN, TWO SIDES—$1.99, I think, "Four to six? I gotta come back for that."

If the early-bird triggers that response, you're old.

Another sign that tells you that you've turned fifty is memory loss. I hate it when I'm with friends and they start getting nostalgic, talking about the good old days, and someone invariably says, "Hey, George, remember when you did this . . . ?" or, "Remember that time when we . . . ? That was hilarious." I smile like an idiot and nod knowingly, even though I have no idea what they're talking about. I'm down to remembering one out of every three stories, at most.

I'm also forgetting where I left things. People try to be helpful. They say, "Where was the last place you put it?"

If I could remember the last place I put it, I would know where it is now. Because the last place I put it is where it is.

The worst is when you actually have the object you're

going to use in your hand, and you don't know what it's doing there or what you were about to do with it.

"I see the phone in my hand, but who was I gonna call?"

I guess a sure sign of dementia would be looking at the phone in your hand and saying, "What is this in my hand? What the hell am I supposed to do with it? What does this thing do?"

I also think—and this scares me the most—that I'm going blind because I text too much. I'm sure an FDA study will be coming out any minute telling us that texting causes blindness. The other day I got a beep indicating that I had a new text message. I picked up my phone and looked at the screen . . . and I could not read it. It was too blurry and too small. I squinted at it. I brought the phone an inch from my face. Didn't help. Then I moved my head back, stretched my arms out as far as I could. Made no difference. I turned the phone to the left, to the right, and upside down. I still could not read the text. I got very frustrated.

"I can't read this, you stupid piece of *shit*!" I shouted, which was not cool, because I was in a restaurant.

I gave in. I fumbled in my bag for my glasses, which are progressives, found them, and put them on. I read the text, saw it clearly. It was from my friend RJ. I called RJ to tell him the sad news.

"I need a new phone," I said.

"Why? You just got that phone."

"I couldn't read the text you sent me. What did you do, put it in some tiny midget font to mess with me?"

"I didn't do anything to the font. It's your eyes."

"What are you talking about? My eyes are twenty-twenty. And I just paid a fortune for these fancy glasses."

RJ hesitated. I could tell he was trying to think of a delicate way to break some bad news to me.

"George," he said. "Your eyes are . . . old. You're getting old man's eyes."

"Old man's eyes, my ass. It's this texting. If you text, you go blind. They just did a study—"

"Come on. There's no study."

"Fine," I said. "I made up the study. But there should be a study."

"Face it, George. You're over fifty. Your body is starting to go."

"My body is starting to go," I mumbled. "Is that all you got to say?"

"No," he said. "Welcome to the club."

# BITE ME

**ONE** morning, I looked at myself in the bathroom mirror, smiled, and made a decision.

"That's it. I'm getting my teeth fixed."

I was finally gonna do it. I'd lived with Stonehenge in my mouth for fifty years, and I'd had enough.

My mouth was a mess and getting worse. My gums had receded all the way to Reseda. My receding gums had caused my teeth to start caving in on themselves. A couple of my front teeth looked like crossed swords. Then I noticed that whenever somebody took my picture, my bottom teeth cast a dark, foreboding shadow. Not good when you spend a lot of your life in front of a camera.

I'd put off dealing with my teeth before, because I'm not that crazy about fifty-year-olds with braces. Especially when I'm the one walking around with the grille. That's not a good look for me. I refused to leave the house looking like an oversize sixth-grade science nerd or the Mexican version of Flavor Flav.

As a kid, I let my teeth go. It was partly cultural. Going to the dentist was never a high priority for our family. It was too expensive and just not something you did. Plus it was a pain in the ass when I did go, because the dentist always found a ton of cavities. He gave me crap when I told him that I slept all night with a piece of candy in my mouth. Like that was a bad thing.

When I reached middle school, I started to become self-conscious about my bottom teeth, because they were a little crooked. One in particular was not only crooked; it was shorter than the others. I hated that. Made me feel like a freak. I decided to ask my grandmother about getting braces, but then something happened at school that changed my mind: Girls noticed me. And here's the weird part: They thought my teeth were cute.

"Ooh," they said, "it's so adorable how your little tooth is kind of crooked. It gives you such character."

I couldn't fix my teeth after that. Forget it. I had to stay cute.

Then my little tooth kept growing. And growing. It kept growing until it became a fang. Suddenly girls no longer called me adorable or said I had character. They stopped talking to me at all. One day I brought up the idea of braces to my grandmother.

"Braces? You kidding me? Your teeth are so adorable."

It took several years, until I was out of school, but I finally decided to pay more attention to my teeth. I made an appointment with a dentist, a guy RJ recommended. One thing about RJ: Dude has good teeth.

"Go to my guy," he said. "He'll fix you up."

So I went. The dentist spent about an hour going over my teeth, poking around, and peering into my mouth with that little handheld mirror. The whole time he kept shaking his head and muttering, "Wow, yeah, huh," and occasionally, "Ooh, wow, damn." Finally, he snapped off that big overhead lamp, the one that makes you want to confess all the bad stuff you've done in your life, folded his hands in his lap, and said, "I'll be straight with you. In ten years, your teeth are going to start to go."

I fidgeted in my chair. I wanted to make sure I heard him right. "What do you mean by my teeth are gonna *go*? Where? Where are they going?"

"You're going to lose them."

"All of them?"

He sat back in his chair and paused. He chose his words carefully. "Think about it this way," he said. "Pretend your mouth is a house. One day the ceiling starts to crack. Suddenly, a month or two later, the whole roof falls in and you can't even stand up."

"So, my ceiling's starting to crack?"

"Yes. It's cracking. You need to come back as soon as possible. We have to get to work."

Now I folded my hands. "All right. You convinced me. I'm in. I'm gonna come back and patch up that ceiling."

I didn't go back.

Until I turned fifty.

Sickened by the shadow of my smile, disgusted by my disaster of a mouth, I decided that once and for all, I had to fix my teeth. I sucked it up and went back to that same dentist.

"Remember me?" I said.

"Long time between appointments," he said.

"I got freaked out. But I'm ready now. I just hope that the roof of my mouth house hasn't fallen in yet."

"Let's take some X-rays and we'll go from there."

He called in his hygienist, who jammed this alien, space-age thing that looked like a big nose up against my cheek. She then draped a heavy bib over my chest to prevent me from getting zapped with radioactivity. As soon as she had the bib in place, she sprinted out of the room. I thought, "All they got to protect me against deadly gamma rays is an extra-large bib? Seems wrong. She should have to stay in here, too."

After she came back in and moved that alien nose to the other side of my face, then under my chin, and removed the bib—running out of the room every time—she snapped the X-rays she had developed onto some clips on the wall. Then the dentist came in and spent what seemed like forever staring into my mouth with his little hand mirror. Finally, he flicked off the overhead lamp and again sat on his chair and folded his hands in his lap the same way he had fifteen years before.

"Okay," he said.

"I'm *okay?*" I said. "Yes! Thank God!"

"No, I mean, 'Okay, we have to redo the whole thing.'"

"Everything? My whole mouth? All my teeth?"

"I'm afraid so."

"I've been flossing. I flossed twice yesterday."

He shook his head. "I'm sorry."

I sagged into my chair. "What happened?"

He shrugged. "You got old."

"See what happens when you turn fifty?" I thought. "It all goes to hell."

The dentist stood up and walked to the photos of my teeth that the hygienist had clipped to the wall. He slapped at the picture of my whole bottom row. "You've got a ton of silver fillings," he said. "That's like putting asbestos in your mouth. Nobody does silver fillings anymore. And the rest of your teeth, well . . ."

"So, the whole roof caved in, huh?"

"Put it this way," the dentist said. "If your mouth were a building, it would've been condemned."

"I used that little rubber-tipped thing, too—"

He shook his head again, gravely. Now I folded my hands in my lap. I was resigned. I wasn't going anywhere this time. "Okay, I'm in," I said. "How much is this gonna cost? Roughly."

He paused. "You like cars, right?"

"Yes."

"Think about it this way: We'll be putting a seven-series BMW into your mouth."

"Can't we test-drive a Honda?"

He shrugged and shook his head at the same time.

"You're killing me," I said.

"When your mouth gets dirty, you get decay, your gums go, and you have constant bad breath. All that happens when you get older."

"You're really making my day. You got any good news?"

"See that nurse out there?"

I craned my neck and caught a glimpse of a very unattractive bear of a woman in a green uniform that looked as if it was about to burst.

"Don't tell me," I said. "The good news is—"

"Yes," the dentist said. "I'm not screwing her."

In the end, the dentist overhauled all my teeth in two relatively quick, relatively painless appointments.

First, he took molds. The hygienist shoved my bottom teeth into a sticky, mushy, gooey mixture that looked like oatmeal and tasted like a combination of plaster and bad hummus. She tapped me on the shoulder and I pulled my bottom teeth out of that goo, and then she shoved my top teeth into the same yummy crap. When she finished making the molds, the dentist gave me a shot and knocked me out.

While I slept, she and the dentist scanned my teeth, cleaned them, drilled them, filed them, and fitted them with plastic temporaries and mouthpieces. I came to with my dentist's hairy fingers in my mouth.

"He's awake. Okay, almost done. In two weeks, you'll be wearing your brand-new set of teeth."

"Umgraybum."

"Terrific. Tell me if this hurts."

"Gwantawaggamumba."

"Great! Okay."

He removed his fingers and smiled down at me. "I'll see you in two weeks. Don't forget."

"I promise I won't blow off that appointment. I can't. You have my teeth."

Two weeks later, I sat in the same dentist's chair and

waited. Within a few minutes, the dentist came in hold-ing a wooden box the size of a cigar box. "You ready?" he said.

I nodded.

The dentist slowly opened the lid of the box.

Inside was a mouth.

Filled with gleaming gorgeous white teeth.

My teeth.

"Wow," I said.

"These are yours," the dentist said.

"It's so freaky. I feel like I'm in some weird horror movie."

"I think they look terrific," the dentist said.

"They're perfect," I said. "They look like Chiclets, only better."

"Shall we?" he said.

"Yes."

A nurse waved in an anesthesiologist, who set up and then injected me with a dose of propofol, the stuff that killed Michael Jackson. That was a terrible tragedy, a senseless loss, but I have to say, this propofol was unbeliev-able. I felt peaceful and zonked and . . . *young*. The drug made me feel fifteen years old again. And incredibly rested. No wonder this shit is so dangerous.

When I woke up, I felt strange and I felt different.

The dentist lowered the large overhead mirror in front of me and I stared at myself. I blinked. I didn't rec-ognize the face in the mirror. Then slowly I recognized my nose, my eyes, and my cheeks, and I realized it was me. But, man, I felt like a new person.

Because I had a whole new mouth.

I'd heard some people say that having veneers made them feel insecure.

I had the exact opposite reaction. I felt totally secure. I loved how I looked, and I no longer felt embarrassed to smile. I wanted to smile all the time. I wanted to walk around like a grinning maniac. I wanted to ask strangers to take my picture. I was hoping that I would be recognized just so I could show people my new teeth.

The point is, if there is something wrong with you, you need to deal with it, and soon. Do not wait. Go to your dentist or your doctor and get your problem looked at. And go regularly so that they can keep an eye on you. It's not cool to say, "I've been pissing blood, but, screw it, I didn't go to the doctor. I'm fine. I haven't been to the doctor in nineteen years."

Yeah, tough guy.

Don't take pride in shit like that.

That is no badge of honor.

That's like saying, "Yeah, my husband's been beating the crap out of me for twenty-two years, but we're still married!"

You know what? You shouldn't be. You should be gone, and your husband should be locked in a jail cell with several inmates named Killer.

# MY LEFT FOOT, I MEAN, MY RIGHT KIDNEY

IN my forties, I was diagnosed with kidney disease. My first reaction was not, "Oh, no!" or, "Why me?"

It was, "Why not?"

I thought, "Sure. That makes sense. What's the worst that can happen? Whatever it is, it'll happen to me."

I wasn't being a doomsayer, and I wasn't saying, "Oh, woe is me." Not at all. At that point in my life, I was just used to experiencing a continuous series of worst-case scenarios coming true. You know in *Peanuts* when Lucy keeps picking up the football every time Charlie Brown runs up to kick it? That was me. Not Charlie Brown. The football.

So, yeah, I was used to bad news.

February 2005.

Cedars-Sinai Medical Center in Los Angeles.

I have kidney disease. That much we know. What I don't know is how bad. I know it's bad enough that I need a transplant—I'm scheduled to receive a kidney in April—but can I make it through the remaining weeks of production for *The George Lopez Show*? Hell, will I make it through the rest of the *day*?

Nobody knows how sick I am.

*I* don't even know how sick I am.

I walk into the lab at Cedars for an ultrasound, a scan of my back. The technician grins when he sees me. We exchange a few words in Spanish. He laughs as he rubs the gel on my back. The gel is cold. I jump a little and make a joke in Spanish. The tech laughs again. He reaches over for the wand attached to the ultrasound machine and rolls it in a circle on my back. He starts to say something else, but stops abruptly, right in the middle of a sentence. He slowly rolls the wand, but now he looks away from me and stares off at the ultrasound machine. A pall hangs over the room. The technician says nothing more. He completes the scan in stony silence. He wipes off the gel and smiles at me, but we both know what awaits me in the doctor's office on the other side of the door.

The worst-case scenario.

I enter the doctor's office and take a chair opposite him. He's tall, white haired, distinguished-looking. He has a reputation for being one of the best kidney specialists in the world, but I've been warned that he lacks a warm bedside manner. He's blunt, to the point. He has no talent for small talk.

"I read your scan," he says. I expect him to tell me there's good news and bad news.

"I have to tell you, you're a walking miracle."

For one precious moment, I leap out of my skin. I'm wrong. He has only good news. No. He has *great* news.

"It's a miracle you're walking at all."

I feel my entire body collapse into itself.

"Your kidneys don't even show up on the ultrasound. They're not *there*. It's like they don't exist."

"That can't be good," I say.

"It's not," he says. "Are you urinating?"

"Yes."

"Good. If you do not urinate for a day, or a day and a half at most, drop everything you're doing and get right in here."

"I have six more shows to shoot—"

"I don't care. If you stop urinating, that means your kidneys are shutting down. You understand how serious this is?"

"Worst-case," I say.

"Correct. You have two months until your transplant. You have to make it until then."

I somehow make it. Each day is torturous. I live every moment with one question hanging over me like an executioner's ax: "How long has it been since I've peed?"

*Pee or die.*

That becomes my mantra, the bumper sticker inside my brain.

I live in a state of exhaustion and fear.

No matter how much I sleep, I wake up wasted.

The toxins swirling around in my body affect my memory. I have to memorize my lines in the remaining six scripts we have

> ## *PEE OR DIE.* THAT BECOMES MY MANTRA, THE BUMPER STICKER INSIDE MY BRAIN.

to shoot and I get lost, confused, the words coming at me in a blur, jumbled up. I manage to make it through the first episode, barely get through the second, then the third, ticking off each one like a prisoner counting off days on death row.

I have no energy. I struggle to perform the simplest tasks. Shaving, showering, sipping tea become monumentally painful chores.

I try to come to peace with what may happen.

I tell myself, "If I don't make it, then, okay, I wasn't meant to go on. I'll accept it. I have to. What's my choice?"

I want to pray for my life, but I'm uncomfortable asking for things.

Then, somehow, I make it through the end of the season.

We shoot the final show.

I manage to keep my disease a secret.

I check into the hospital April 19.

I have my surgery April 20.

When I wake up the morning of April 21, two overpowering and completely new feelings fill me up.

I feel better than I have ever felt in my life.

I know that my life has forever changed.


I was born with extremely narrow ureters. The ureters are the tubes that deliver urine from the kidneys to the bladder. Picture a wide four-lane superhighway. Those would be normal-size ureters. My ureters were like a bike path on the side of the road. I could never figure out exactly why this happened. Eventually somebody in my family told me that I was born early. I guess my ureters never got a chance to develop fully.

The result of my narrow ureters was that I wet the bed. Not just when I was a baby. Always.

Of course, in our culture you could never admit that you wet the bed. We can never admit shit like that. You can't reveal that there's anything wrong with you. You could be coughing up blood and instead of telling anybody, you just say, "Excuse me," and leave the room. We go right into denial. We believe that we're tougher than any disease. We're not gonna let a little thing like coughing up blood or wetting the bed stop us from living our lives.

"I've been coughing up blood for, like, lemme see, one, two . . . six years. No. Seven. Yes. Seven years. But I'm not gonna let it get to me."

Over time, it will get to you.

Time is the boss, not Bruce Springsteen.

**WHEN** I was a kid, I wet the bed every night. I couldn't control myself. My grandmother thought it was because I drank too much water. Yes, she, too, was in denial. She refused to believe that I could be sick, or that, even worse, there might be something seriously wrong with me. I would wake up with the mattress all wet and I would sheepishly tell my grandmother.

"Grandma, the mattress is all wet."

"So turn it over."

She just couldn't deal with it. So I would pee the bed and turn the mattress over, pee the bed, turn the mattress over. My mattress got so wet and nasty that it looked like cinnamon French toast.

I never slept through the night. I would dream of being in water—playing in rivers and rain showers and fountains and waterfalls and running through sprinklers and playing with hoses and splashing in swimming pools— and I'd wake up having peed the bed. I had to joke about it. I told people that my grandmother said, "Growing up, George used to wet the bed," and I said, "Yeah, it was the only hot water we had."

We ignored the danger signs. I know. It seems obvious that something was definitely wrong, especially as I got older and still wet the bed, but my grandparents were simply not conditioned to go to doctors. They were conditioned to tough it out. They were always in bad health. They never watched what they ate or exercised, and I'm sure they were under a ton of stress to make ends meet.

It all caught up with them. My grandfather died when I was twenty-seven. He had a weak heart and was short of breath all the time. Finally, he had an angioplasty. The doctors told him not to walk until he recovered, because he could clot. He didn't listen. Or he misheard. Or he didn't understand. "Yes, they said walk. I'm sure. They told me to *walk*."

The first day back from the hospital he walked, he

clotted, the clot got loose, he went to his room, lay down, and died. Boom. Just like that. Poor guy.

People fear what they don't understand. So, rather than deal with my bed-wetting, my grandparents ignored it, insisted that I drank too much water, and let it go at that. I don't blame them. They didn't know.

It reminds me of people who continue to drive their cars after the warning light comes on. The light appears on the dashboard glowing bright fire-engine red and they ignore it. What do they think, that the car is gonna run forever and that the blazing red light doesn't mean anything? Then when the car breaks down, they say, "I'm so pissed off. I have to replace the entire transmission. I can't believe it."

"Wow. Really?"

"Yes. It turns out I was driving the car for three months without any water. No water at all. Bone-dry. Piece-of-junk car."

"Didn't the red light come on?"

"Yeah, but I thought that meant *service soon*."

Same thing happens with our bodies. We are equipped with warning signs: pain and lumps and knots and bulges and bleeding and, yes—

Wetting the bed.

I kept wetting the bed through elementary school, into junior high, and into high school. I tried to control it— and sometimes I did—but I knew that wetting the bed as a teenager was not normal. By then I was too embarrassed to tell anyone. I dealt with it. I covered it up. It became my dirty little secret.

The first time a doctor noticed something a little unusual was in high school, when I took the physical for the baseball team. I'd had physicals before and always passed, no problem, and nothing ever came up about my bedwetting. I always felt uncomfortable, though. I was worried that somehow I'd get busted.

Senior year my high school brought in a doctor to conduct the physicals, a bored-looking older guy with a salt-and-pepper beard. He wore a sport jacket and a button-down shirt and draped a stethoscope around his neck like a tie. I'd say he was dressed a little fancy for our school. He conducted each physical slowly and deliberately, as if he had nowhere else to go, ever, which, looking at him, was probably true.

This guy was wasting our time. We were athletes, eighteen years old and in peak condition. Getting a physical seemed stupid and unnecessary, not to mention humiliating. We began by stripping down to our underwear and stepping onto an industrial scale. The doctor held a clipboard and wrote down our weight, then pulled up a metal tape measure attached to the back of the scale and scribbled down our height. Then he put his clipboard aside and listened to our chest with his stethoscope. Last, he told us to drop our drawers. We looked up to the ceiling as he cupped our balls and asked us to cough while he checked for a hernia. I was tempted to say, "One more second and you have to buy me flowers," but I thought it was probably a good idea to shut up while he had my balls in his palm.

Then we went back into the locker room, put on everything but our shirts, and came back out so he could take our blood pressure. This was the most boring part, because it took the longest: two minutes. We took this opportunity to fuck around—rag on one another, laugh, call one another out. The bored bearded doctor paid no attention, ignoring us as he went about taking our blood pressure.

I took my place in line and waited as the doctor nodded his approval to all the other guys on the team and dismissed them. I watched them head into the locker room to finish getting dressed. Finally, my turn. I stepped up to a chair that had a desktop attached and sat down. I stretched my arm out on the desktop and looked away as the bored bearded doctor wrapped the blood-pressure cuff around my arm. He squeezed the bubble tight, waited, then released it and watched the meter rise and fall. "Hmm," he said. He seemed alarmed.

"What? What's the matter?"

"Your pressure's a little high."

Time stood still. All he said was, "Your pressure's a little high," but his words sounded ominous and as if they were coming from far away.

It felt like an eternity before he spoke again. "I want you to go outside," he said. "Sit down for a few minutes and then come back in. I'm going to take your blood pressure again."

"*Shit,*" I thought.

"Okay," I said.

I stood up slowly and, head down, went outside. I knew everybody was looking at me. I was the only one on the team who hadn't passed the blood pressure test. I kept my head down, as if I'd flunked an exam or gotten caught screwing around in class.

I found a seat on the bench near the dugout. I didn't know where to look, so I studied the grass in front of me. I didn't know how, but I knew that somehow my high blood-pressure reading was connected to my wetting the bed. I also knew that I was I too scared to mention anything about that.

After a while I went back inside, took my place in line again, and stepped up for my second blood-pressure test.

The doctor wrapped my arm in the blood-pressure cuff and squeezed the bubble tighter this time, I thought. He seemed to be moving in slow motion. The two minutes felt like twenty. Finally, he released the balloon and squinted at the meter. "It went down a little," he said.

I felt a huge wave of relief.

"But . . ."

"What?"

I thought he was about to say something else, but he stopped. He nodded slowly. "Nothing," he said. "You're all right."

Of course, I wasn't all right.

Kidney disease creates high blood pressure.

That's one of the signs.

But the doctor didn't allow himself to consider that

worst-case scenario. Or maybe he looked at me, saw a healthy-looking eighteen-year-old kid, a baseball player, and thought, "There can't be anything wrong with him. What are the odds?"

I put on the rest of my uniform, grabbed my glove, and went out to the outfield to shag flies.

I escaped.

But just for the moment.

I dismissed the doctor's reaction. I didn't think about it. I didn't pursue it. I didn't say, "Man, I'm eighteen years old, an athlete, and I have high blood pressure? What's with that?" No. I didn't go there. Besides, who would I tell? My grandparents had conditioned me to tough it out, to battle through pain or discomfort and ignore any potential warning signs. I've never figured out if my grandparents didn't trust doctors or if they were afraid of what they would find out if they went to a doctor. Maybe a little of both. Anyway, I kept moving forward, continued pushing on.

By the time I reached my twenties, I wet the bed less frequently and then almost not at all. But by my late twenties, I started to feel fatigued at the end of every day. Every morning I woke up tired no matter how much I'd slept. I chalked that up to overworking. I was busting my ass, going on the road, working at club after club, honing my act. It paid off. My career started to catch fire. Late-night talk shows began to notice me. Then, in 1991, when

I was thirty, the booker from *The Arsenio Hall Show* called and offered me a spot. A big break.

As I sat in the green room waiting to go on with Arsenio, I felt unusually warm. Sweat pooled under my arms, on my neck, and then I felt that the back of my neck was drenched. I stood up. My knees felt rubbery. I took a step and the room started spinning. The door flew open and the stage manager burst in, shouting back at a thin, metallic voice that squawked at her through her headset. She pointed at me, then wheeled her arm in a circle like a third-base coach waving in a runner. I was on. I followed her to the stage, desperately trying to keep my balance. She steered me to my spot on the stage. Lights above me flicked on, their high beams drilling me, baking me. Rivers of sweat poured off me. I heard Arsenio's introduction and the audience's applause and I began my set. I somehow made it through, the distant sound of laughter and applause bouncing vaguely around me. I went straight home after the show, stripped off my sweat-soaked clothes, and took my temperature. I had a high fever. I drove myself to the doctor the next day, and he gave me his diagnosis: pneumonia. He prescribed antibiotics, and in a couple weeks I was back to normal. Normal, that is, for me.

What the doctor didn't realize was that pneumonia can be a side effect of kidney disease.

He would have found that out if he had done a full blood panel.

Which, of course, he didn't.

SEVEN years later.

I'm constantly fatigued, due, I'm sure, to my ferocious work schedule. I refuse to complain or cut back. I live to work.

One morning I wake up with a dull pain in my lower right side. I pop some Advil. The pills have no effect. I pop some more. The pain persists through the day, making it hard for me to walk. I work through the pain, hoping that it will go away. Basically, I approach the dull pain in my side the way I always approach pain and discomfort: I ignore it.

After a while, the pain lessens but I start to become fatigued. I drag my ass to Canada to play some club dates. A friend tells me about some supplements he heard about that increase your energy, which happen to be illegal in the United States. I find them for sale in bulk in a bin at a Canadian pharmacy. I buy a bagful, down a couple, and feel my energy amp up instantly.

I go to Las Vegas to play a weeklong gig at a major hotel on the Strip. I keep taking the supplements, but lower the number. My appetite decreases. I find that I'm constantly thirsty and I have to pee seemingly every five minutes. One night, I finish my first of several sold-out shows—a challenge, because I have to pee the whole time I'm onstage. I rush to the bathroom in the club, the crowd's applause breaking like a wave at my back, and position myself at the closest urinal. I start to pee and I gasp.

My piss is purple.

At first I think I'm pissing blood, but I realize I've never seen purple blood. "What the hell is that?" I say.

I move in tighter to the urinal to make sure nobody can see what's happening. I look away, hoping that maybe I'm hallucinating; maybe it's something in those supplements, but I've cut way back on those. I think maybe it was something I had for dinner, but I don't recall eating any purple food, can't even think of any purple food. . . . Wait—eggplant, plums, grapes, licorice, cauliflower . . . have I had any of those? I look back down. . . .

And I'm still pissing purple.

"Damn, I'm pissing *purple*."

Of course, it's obvious what I will do the moment I finish pissing purple.

Nothing.

I do nothing.

I don't tell anyone.

I don't go to the doctor.

I should have gone to the doctor. I know that.

But I have shows to do.

And I think I had some baba ghanoush the other night. It was probably bad. Tainted baba ghanoush. Yeah. That's what caused the purple pee. Must have been.

After a couple of days, I stop pissing purple. Just like that. No more violet whiz. That must mean everything's okay, right?

No. Of course not. Purple piss must mean *something*. And that something cannot be good. Doesn't matter. I ignore this warning sign, this bright, flashing, blinking, deep purple indicator light. I pretend that I never saw it.

I finish playing Vegas and hit the road for a series of club dates in Texas. San Antonio. Houston. Austin. I'm killing every night.

And every day I feel like I'm dying.

The pain in my side returns.

Only worse.

The dull ache becomes a constant, jabbing pain. It feels as if someone has stabbed me in the side with a butcher knife.

The fatigue returns.

I spend my days soaking in baths to soothe the pain, or zonked out in bed trying to sleep.

I stop taking the energy supplements, replacing them with a regimen of Advil.

I keep working. Half the time when I perform, my head's in a cloud, my words blurred by the pain that burns my side. The audience doesn't notice.

Then one day I tear my Achilles tendon.

I limp for weeks, the injury refusing to heal. Back in Los Angeles, I go to a wound care center. They extract some of my blood, spin it, make a serum, and apply it to the tear. My Achilles heals.

But I can't stand up.

The pain in my side is so severe it bends me over.

Finally, I do what I should have done years before.

I go to the doctor.

I see the same doctor who diagnosed my pneumonia seven years earlier.

When he sees that I can't stand up, he looks at me with what I see as deep concern.

He checks me over completely.

He takes a full blood panel.

I come back the next day for a follow-up visit and to receive the blood work results. Walking like a ninety-year-old caveman, I follow a nurse down a corridor past a row of examining rooms, and into his office. I sit in a leather chair across from the doctor's desk. A few minutes later, the doctor comes in holding my chart. He closes the door behind him and sits at his desk. He absently flicks the corner of my chart.

I feel like shit.

He looks like shit.

He may look even worse than I do.

"I have bad news," he says.

"So much for the foreplay," I think.

"You have kidney disease, and it's pretty advanced."

I squirm in the chair, the leather squishing as I try to find a comfortable position. I'm biding time, trying to digest what the doctor has said.

Kidney disease.

"Sure," I think. "Why not? Of all the crap that's happened to me, why the hell not? Why wouldn't I have kidney disease? Makes perfect sense. Of course."

He lowers his voice, clears his throat. "You're going to need a transplant before you're forty-five."

I'm thirty-eight.

"Okay," I say, exhaling softly. "So I have seven years—"

"It doesn't work like that. You're going to deteriorate every year. I'm going to be on you now, watching you carefully, checking you, measuring your kidney function, but you've got to start thinking about lining up a donor now. You will get worse and worse. I'm going to prescribe medication for you today, right now, but it's going to get a lot worse."

I wish I had gone to him sooner.

I wish he had noticed the kidney disease seven years earlier, when I came in with pneumonia.

I wish . . .

Well, it doesn't matter.

Getting angry, getting depressed, getting even . . .

Those emotions don't help.

Dealing with it.

That can help.

Which is what I did.

I made it until I was forty-four. I survived that season of *The George Lopez Show*. I made it through in one piece, upright . . . barely. At my last examination the doctor told me that I had a total of eighteen percent function in *both* kidneys.

As I lay in that hospital bed before my transplant, a million thoughts swirled through my mind. The first words that came into my head were, "Well, this is where the rubber meets the road." I'd never said that before in my life. I'm naked, scared, about to go under the knife, and suddenly I became an old white guy. Then I thought about dying and about all the things I hadn't yet accomplished. But mainly I thought about how lucky I was and how precious time is. Time is a gift. Especially if you're over fifty. People waste too much time on nothing. I hear people saying all the time, "I'm thinking about going to Hawaii next year."

Why wait? Go this year. You don't know what's gonna happen next year. Do not assume you're going to live to a ripe old age. You're already pretty damn old. Grab things now.

I also thought about how my fear of doctors nearly killed me.

Listen, this is not a self-help book, not even close, but help yourself to this one piece of advice:

If you're afraid of doctors, get over it.

If you hate physical exams, or colonoscopies or prostate exams, get over it. I'm not gonna lie: When that doctor shoves his rubber-covered finger up your ass, it's gonna hurt, unless you're used to it. But if he finds something that shouldn't be up there, like a half of an apple or an old iPhone or a tumor, you're gonna thank him.

I also thought about all the warning signs I saw that I did nothing about.

You have to learn to accept this fact:

*Your body is your best friend.*

I know. You're thinking, "Hey, my best friend lives in Wisconsin."

No, he doesn't. He lives inside of you. Your best friend

in Wisconsin is not gonna know that you've been hacking in your sleep.

Don't do what I did. Don't ignore those warning signs. See a doctor right away.

And never ignore purple urine.

# GOLF LESSONS

**THE** moment I turned fifty, I started contemplating the future. Let's face it: At my age, you need to make choices. Lifestyle choices. I started thinking about things that never would have entered my consciousness ten years ago, even five years ago, foreign concepts such as "slowing down," "drinking less," and "having sex once a week."

I even toyed with the idea of retirement.

Not immediately, but possibly in ten years. I could definitely see that. The road's a grind, man. Performing in clubs, finishing a set at two o'clock in the morning night after night, flying to the next city, trying to get your bearings, fighting jet lag, keeping your energy high, and then starting all over at another club in another city until another two a.m. It's wearing me down at fifty. It could kill me at sixty. I can see how retirement might be appealing. As unbelievable as it may seem, I can foresee a time in the not-so-distant future when I might give up performing.

But I'll never give up golf.

When I die, I either want to go in my sleep or after sinking a thirty-foot birdie putt.

I don't just love golf. I *am* golf. It's in my DNA.

Without a doubt, I am happiest and most relaxed when I'm on a golf course. When I finish a round, it's hard for me to leave. I like to hang out at the clubhouse afterward and have a drink with the guys, chilling and watching other guys playing golf. If I have nothing else to do after that, I'll go home and watch a golf match or the Golf Channel. It doesn't stop there. At night, to relax, I sneak off to my secret undisclosed location and take out my special box of tees, balls, and ball markers that I've accumulated over the years. I climb into bed, turn over the box, and dump out all the contents. I sift through all my tees and markers—my cherished mementos—look them over, polish them, and put them carefully back into the box, one by one.

One time my girlfriend came in and caught me sorting my tees and markers. I didn't hear her walk in, and I don't know how long she stood in the doorway watching me, because I was too engrossed going through my tee stash.

"What are you doing?" she said.

She didn't sound happy. In fact, she sounded a little put out, as if she'd caught me in bed with another woman instead of a box of tees.

"I'm going through my tees and markers."

"You're sorting your old golf tees?"

"And markers. It relaxes me. What's the problem?"

"No problem. It just seems a little . . . unusual."

"Well, I can do this or I can watch porn."

"No, no, have a good time. Okay, well, I'm gonna get ready for bed. Think I'll have a glass of wine, take a bath, maybe slip into something more comfortable, like that new nightgown, in case, you know, you might want to—"

"Is it Wednesday already?"

She left. I waited about ten seconds before I packed up all my tees and markers and got ready to go after her. I filled the box up and started to get off the bed when my hand brushed against a golf ball that had rolled under my pillow. I picked it up and looked at it. It had a picture of Bugs Bunny on it.

"My Looney Tunes golf balls," I said.

I remembered the day not that long ago that I ended up with a package of golf balls with a different Looney Tunes character painted on each one. I decided to play a round with one.

I teed up Bugs Bunny on the first hole at my local course. I hadn't played in a while and I felt a little rusty. I probably should've hit a bucket before playing a round, but I didn't. I jumped right in.

I decided to play it safe and hit my drive with a three iron. I swung and immediately knew I shanked my shot. I looked up and Bugs Bunny flew in a line over the fence to my right and bounced into a construction site.

"Damn," I said. "I hit poor Bugs sideways. Let's see what I do with Yosemite Sam."

I got into my stance and hit my second drive.

*Crraaank.*

"Whoa. There goes Sam."

Yosemite Sam sailed over the fence and banged off a bulldozer.

"I can't shank all of them," I said. "Wile E. Coyote. Come on, man."

I swung and hit the three iron.

I might as well have been *facing* the damn fence.

Wile E. Coyote landed two feet away from Bugs.

"This is ridiculous. I can't hit all six over. Come on, Tweety Bird; straighten your feathery little ass out."

*Whack.*

Shanked in a line over the fence.

"Well, I know this: I hold the record for hitting the most consecutive Looney Tunes characters into a construction site."

Normally, at that point I would have felt somewhere between trying to bottle up my frustration and not scream at the top of my lungs and about to throw my clubs over the fence after the Looney Tunes balls, but as I watched Tweety Bird clang around the construction site, I started to laugh.

"All right, Sylvester, are you gonna go down the fairway or chase Tweety Bird?"

I swung.

He went after Tweety.

I held the next Looney Tunes ball in my hand and stared at it.

Speedy Gonzales.

"Speedy, it's you and me, brother. Do not let me down. Do not join your cartoon brothers. Go straight down the fairway. Prove your Mexican mettle. I want to see your loyalty."

I teed up Speedy, slowed my swing way down, and concentrated on not lifting my head or pulling my shot.

*Whacccckkkkk.*

"Yes! That felt so good. . . . *No!* Not you, too, Speedy. Nooo!"

He flew over the fence and nestled right up next to Bugs Bunny.

"Really, Speedy? What are you doing going after Bugs? I knew it. You two are gay!"

Six Looney Tunes balls over the fence. Two more left. Taz Devil and a second Bugs Bunny. I shook my head. I smiled, placed Taz on a tee, stuck him into the ground, and walked off the course, laughing. I put Bugs in my pocket. As a result of my worst driving exhibition ever, Bugs the Second earned a cherished spot in my box of mementos.

Golf Lesson Number One:

Some days just suck. The only thing you can change about that is your attitude.

On those days, if you can, laugh.

IT doesn't matter who you are—how rich or how powerful—golf does not discriminate. The game is an equal opportunity torturer. I've played with Donald Trump, and as wealthy as he is, he could not buy a par.

The game not only tests your will and patience; you

also have to factor in several outside forces. The course itself, for one. In basketball, for example, it doesn't matter where you play; the court is always the same size. A twenty-foot jump shot in L.A. is still a twenty-foot jump shot in Boston or Miami. In golf, every hole you play is different, not only on every course, but on the same course. Plus you have to deal with all sorts of complications and distractions—sand traps, water hazards, trees, rough, wind, the glare of the sun, the cut of the grass, the placement of the pin, slow players, fast players, players who wear loud pants or clothes that don't match or stupid hats.

Ultimately, I think that golf is an addiction. It sucks you in and then grabs hold of you and won't let you go. I've heard experts say that the reason people get addicted to drugs like cocaine and heroin is that they are always chasing that first high. Same with golf. When you hit a great shot, a sensation runs through your entire body, pulsing up from the face of the club all the way into your chest. It's a deep feeling of joy and power.

Once you get that feeling—especially the first time—you jones to get it again. You can't wait to hit your next shot. And if the next time you swing, you top the ball and it trickles ten feet in front of you and rolls into a pond, you can't wait to erase that crappy feeling and take your next swing, hoping to experience that indescribable feeling of joy and power again. You chase that high from swing to swing and from round to round.

If you play a great round, you can't wait for your next round so you can experience those feelings again. If you play a bad round, you can't wait to play again to redeem yourself, always chasing that sensation of joy and power. No doubt: Golf is a high.

Golf is also a great teacher. I think people should give up therapy and take up golf. It's cheaper and more effective. I know I wouldn't be the comedian I turned out to be or the man I am if it weren't for golf.

When I was younger, if I hit a couple of really awful shots in a row, I used to throw the club. I'd curse and wind up and let the club fly. I'd wing it into the bushes and storm off the course. One day, playing in a foursome with RJ, I lost it after nine horrible holes. I dropped my clubs into the rough and headed straight for my car.

"Where you going?" RJ said.

"I'm out."

"What? Come on. We got the back nine to play."

"I'm done, man. I play like crap. I'm *out*. The hell with this."

I got into the car, started it up, and froze. I couldn't move. I sat behind the wheel staring through the windshield, seething, my chest heaving. I said to myself, "What are you doing? You can't keep reacting this way. How you gonna get better if you quit? You've been a quitter your whole life. You gonna quit now, too?"

"No," I said aloud. "I'm gonna stick it out."

I got out of the car, slowly walked back to RJ, and picked up my clubs. "You gotta be a fool to play this stupid game," I said.

"That's true. Or a masochist."

I sighed. "I'll do better on the back nine."

"That wouldn't be hard," he said.

Lesson Number Two:

You can't get better at something if you quit.

I used to spend half my round in the trees. When I swung, I developed a bad habit of leaning back too much. I'd end up pushing my shot to the right. Way to the right. Every time. I'd charge into the woods, find my ball, select a long iron, and hit some crazy-ass shot to try to save par. Even though I'd be in the middle of a damn forest, I'd try to make my ball curl around a tree, or I'd attempt to lift the ball over the top of the trees. I *had* to get on the green. I had to salvage the hole. That's what I thought. Even if I had an impossible lie, I'd go for it. I was insane.

Guess what. The same thing happened every time.

I'd hit my shot, and instead of going around a tree or sailing over the trees, my ball would whack into the tree right in front of me and shoot back at me like a bullet. I'd cover my head and duck to get out of the way. Sometimes I hit the ground. It took me years, but I finally figured out that being so reckless wasn't working. I needed another plan. I realized I had to calm down, slow down, and . . . *play it safe.*

The next time I pushed my ball into the trees, which was pretty much the next time I teed off, I tried something completely different. Instead of hitting some wild, crazy, impossible shot, I took out my pitching wedge and chipped easily out to the fairway. Much less dramatic, but much safer. I didn't get my hat knocked off. Or my head. And I didn't lose two extra strokes.

Yes, I was in trouble, but I accepted it rather than doing something ridiculous that would make it worse. I should've been true to my heritage. Because if there's one thing a Mexican can do, it's get out of trouble.

Lesson Number Three:

If you get in trouble, don't try to do too much. Take the safe way out. You can't fix everything with one wild, dramatic swing.

If you get in trouble, the first thing you have to do is get out of trouble.

**PEOPLE** do some crazy stuff on a golf course.

I once played with a guy, call him Clem, a serious golfer and seriously cheap, who fell in love with a new golf ball that had just come out, call it the Suprema Pro. According to Clem, the Suprema Pro was superball, the greatest golf ball ever made, a duffer's dream. Scientists had supposedly spent years locked away in a laboratory perfecting this golf ball, adding extra dimples so that you'd always hit it straight, and inventing a special core made of Flubber or some magic dust so you'd always add an extra fifty yards to every shot. Of course, you had to pay a premium price for the Suprema Pro, something like nine bucks a ball.

One Sunday, I played Pebble Beach and the starter

paired me up with Clem. In addition to a three-pack of the new Suprema Pros, Clem brought along his five-year-old son, Tommy. Fine with me. Might as well get kids started young.

First hole. Clem teed up his nine-dollar Suprema Pro, waggled his ass like a stripper, wound up, and hit his drive. The ball flew way off to the right, sailed out-of-bounds and over a fence, and landed in someone's backyard right near a swing set.

"Nice shot, Daddy," the kid said.

"I wasn't aiming for the swing set, Tommy. Come on; let's go get that ball. It cost me nine dollars."

He lifted Tommy into the cart and roared off. He drove along the fence, finally stopping at the house with the swing set. His Suprema Pro lay on the other side of the fence, twenty feet away. He parked the golf cart as snugly as he could against the fence.

"Tommy," Clem said, "I want you to get Daddy's ball. I'm gonna lift you over the fence. You run to the ball, pick it up, then run back to the fence, reach your arms up, and I'll bring you back."

The kid stared at his father. He didn't look so sure about this plan.

"It's no big deal," Clem said. "It'll be fun."

Before the kid could say anything, Clem stood up on the seat of the golf cart and picked up Tommy.

"You ready?"

The kid nodded.

"One . . . two . . . three!"

Clem lifted Tommy up and over the fence and gently deposited him into the backyard of the house.

"You see the ball? It's right over there. You can't miss it."

Tommy turned and located the Suprema Pro lying against a metal support of the swing set. "I see it," Tommy mumbled.

"Great! Now go get it!"

Tommy popped his thumb into his mouth, hesitated, sucked up his courage, and walked slowly over to the Suprema Pro. He squatted, picked up the ball, rolled it over in his hands, and examined it.

"That's it! You got it! Now come on back and—"

*RRRRRRAAARRGH!*

A distant rumble that rolled into a horrific growl sent a chill through Clem and Tommy simultaneously. They both froze.

A rottweiler—fangs bared, saliva dripping from wide-open jaws, eyes narrowed and yellow—streaked around the corner of the house, running low and ferociously toward Tommy.

"Uh-oh," Clem said.

"Daddy!"

"Tommy! Run!"

*RRRRRRRAAARGGGGH!*

The rottweiler bared his teeth and charged toward Tommy.

Tommy looked at the Suprema Pro that he held in his hands.

"Tommy, run! Forget the ball! It's okay! I got two more! *Run!*"

A blur of black fur and white fangs.

All Clem could see.

Filling his line of vision.

The rottweiler rushing at Tommy.

Tommy screamed. The ball rolled out of his hands. He lowered his head and raced toward the fence.

He took two steps and fell.

The dog bore down on him.

"I'm putting my son's life in jeopardy for a nine-dollar golf ball," Clem moaned. "Your mother's gonna kill me."

The five-year-old scrambled to his feet and sprinted toward the fence. Flying around the side of the swing set, the rottweiler skidded to avoid the metal support. He opened his mouth, planted his front legs, and leaped at Tommy.

But his right front paw landed on the Suprema Pro.

His legs flew out from under him.

The rottweiler flipped into the air and sprawled onto the ground with a thud—at the same moment Tommy grabbed onto the fence.

The rottweiler righted himself, shook his head, and charged.

Clem threw himself onto the fence on the other side, reached his arms over, and hauled Tommy up, just as the rottweiler chomped at Tommy, missing his ass by an inch, biting the air.

Clem and Tommy landed in the front of the golf cart

and Clem gunned it, the frustrated, hellish howl of the rottweiler at their backs.

"Golf's a hard game," Tommy said with a shiver.

"Sure is," Clem said, and then he muttered under his breath, "Nine bucks for that ball. Damn Cujo."

Lesson Number Four:

Get your priorities straight.

# IMMORTALITY, OR FREEZING MY ASS FOR THE NEXT HUNDRED YEARS

I think about my mortality every day.

Because you never know. This could be it. The end of the line. You can't predict if you're gonna go peacefully in your sleep or if some dude working construction thirty stories up is gonna accidentally knock off a piece of rebar and bash in your skull while you're standing at a corner, sending a text. I knew a guy who was putting up his Christmas lights and fell off his house. Boom. Gone. That's all she wrote.

That's why you have to enjoy life and make the most of every moment. Of course, take care of yourself, but don't go over-the-top. Don't shut yourself down. If you want to have a shot of tequila at two in the afternoon, so what? If you have an urge for a piece of cake, go for it. What are you waiting for? Do it. If that rebar boomerangs out of the sky and clunks you in the head and you're lying on the sidewalk with your life passing before your eyes, you don't want your dying words to be, "I wish I had that piece of cake."

I always keep a box of doughnuts in my house, because when I was a kid, my grandmother didn't allow them in the house. She gave me a million reasons. They were treats, only for special occasions. Or they were bad for you. Or they cost too much. Or I'd abuse my doughnut privilege and eat too many at the same time. Whatever the real reason, I never had any doughnuts when I was growing up. Now, at night, when I'm foraging around the kitchen deciding on a late-night snack, I want to know that I have the option of a doughnut. I never eat them, but I like seeing them there. Makes me feel safe. Gives me comfort.

## IF YOU WANT TO HAVE A SHOT OF TEQUILA AT TWO IN THE AFTERNOON, SO WHAT?

I also don't believe in the saying, "He who dies with the most toys wins." No. He who dies with the most toys has too many toys. And I think we're potentially looking at a selfish hoarder. Get rid of your stuff. Liquidate. I'm on a mission to give a lot of my stuff away. I have accumulated too much—too many cars, watches, golf clubs. I've begun to purge, and it feels great.

This may sound strange, but I feel that getting rid of your excessive crap may be a deeply religious act. Seriously. I would not call myself a religious person. Not at all. If I practice any religion, I would say I'm a member of the House of Golf. But I feel a strong obligation to share, to give my extra stuff away to people who need it more than I do.

The other day I was hanging out at my local coffee shop sipping some tea and reading the paper when I noticed a woman sitting by herself at a table outside. She was a large woman, dressed in shabby clothes, unkempt, obviously homeless. She was staring off, just watching the cars drive by. I could tell she had nowhere to go. She kept staring at the cars with this vacant look in her eyes. But more than that, she looked . . . sad. And lost. And without hope. I don't know what it's like to be homeless, but I recognized that helpless look on her face. I've felt that way myself. Maybe you have, too. You can't seem to take the next step. Or worse, you don't even have the strength to figure out what the next step should be. You just can't get it together. Yes, I've been there.

I got up from my table in the coffee shop, went outside, and walked over to the woman.

"Excuse me," I said. "I don't mean to intrude."

She squinted up at me and shaded her eyes with her hand. I got the feeling that not too many people talked to her politely or with respect.

"How you doing?" I said.

"I'm okay," she said.

"Could you use some financial assistance?"

"Yes," she said. "Yes, I could."

"Okay," I said. "I didn't want to insult you."

I handed her a hundred-dollar bill.

She took it from me without looking at it. She folded up the bill and stuffed it into her pocket. "Thank you," she said.

"You're welcome," I said, and smiled.

Her face brightened, folded into a huge, grateful smile.

That made my day.

I went back into the coffee shop, got my tea and my paper, and sat down. I couldn't get my mind off that woman. I wondered how she'd ended up so destitute, and if she'd use the money to buy food or drugs.

Back in the day, growing up poor and without hope drove a lot of kids to drugs. Now, a lot of rich parents begin medicating their kids at such an early age that by the time they enter middle school, they're already addicts. I call it "parenting by pill."

Some parents don't parent at all.

The worst I've seen are parents who fly to Hawaii or Europe for a vacation and bring their nannies with them. I've been on planes where the only other Latino people have been nannies. I'm sure the parents sold the nanny hard, telling them, "This is gonna be great. We're going to Hawaii. You'll be part of the family." The nanny buys this line for about two minutes, because at the airport she finds out that the rest of the family's flying first-class while she's stuck in coach trying to calm the screaming baby and change his smelly diapers.

It gets even worse once the family hits Waikiki.

While Mom's in the spa and Dad's on the golf course, the nanny's with the kid, entertaining him, changing him, and feeding him out by the pool. First thing in the morning, while the kid and Mom and Dad sleep, the nanny has to rush out and get their cabana all set up. If the nanny has any time to think about it, she'll realize that she might be in Hawaii with the family she works for, but she's the only one who's not on vacation.

This kid will end up so pampered and feeling so privileged that the first time he doesn't get his way, he will completely crumble. If he gets turned down for a job or, more likely, for a highly desirable, nearly impossible-to-get unpaid internship, he will medicate himself to ease the pain of this loss. Let's face it: We've become a medicated society. It's gotten so we can't handle rejection or pain or discomfort—or reality.

I don't know how long I'm gonna live. Nobody does. All I know is that I'm alive today, right now, in this moment, and I feel good. I want to enjoy every second I'm here. I don't ever want to get so old and out of it that if I piss ten cc's, it's a great day. I couldn't bear that.

I used to live next door to a lady who looked around a hundred. She had around-the-clock nursing care. Sometimes a nurse would wheel her outside into the sun and sit with her. Neither one of them said a word. One day, I overheard the nurse talking on her cell phone to the woman's son.

"Oh, yes, it's a great day," the nurse said. "She had a wonderful bowel movement, nice and soft. I'm very proud of her."

Really?

I do not want to end up like that. I don't want to be that incapacitated, and I certainly do not want my bowel movements making anybody proud.

Of course, I don't know if my neighbor took care of herself when she was younger, or if it even matters. Because if taking care of yourself when you're young is that important, then it's pretty much over for me.

Let's start with what doctors now say is one of the single most important activities you can do to assure good health: regular flossing.

Never did it. Nobody in my family flossed. Nobody in my neighborhood flossed. Nobody that I *knew* flossed. Floss? I thought it was a girl's name.

I was so not into flossing that I used to go to sleep with a candy in my mouth. I couldn't wait for the morning, because I knew the moment I woke up I was already eating a candy. I'd keep it tucked in the back of my mouth. I'd wake up, yawn, and think, "Hey, there it is. Oh, yeah. Already starting the day off right."

> **I COULDN'T WAIT FOR THE MORNING, BECAUSE I KNEW THE MOMENT I WOKE UP I WAS ALREADY EATING A CANDY.**

I had two candy preferences. I would sleep with either a chocolate drop tucked back into my mouth or a lemon Jolly Rancher that would attach itself to my teeth. I'd wake up with this delightful fruity taste. I never had to use mouthwash. I had mouthwash built in.

I loved to eat crackers, too. A good cracker went a long way. You'd eat a cracker and some cracker remnant would always get stuck against your back teeth, and then you'd put your finger in your mouth and pull the mushy, mostly eaten cracker remnant forward. So good. It was like you found a second cracker. A dessert cracker. A wonderful surprise.

"George, would you like another cracker?"

"No, thanks, I still got a whole cracker leftover somewhere in my mouth from this morning."

Man, I think about what we did as kids and sometimes I wonder how I made it through my childhood alive. I'm serious. Half the stuff we did back then we've since found out can kill you. Spending more than five minutes outside in the sun, for example. Nobody ever heard about skin cancer–causing UVA rays or UVB rays or SPF to protect you against the UVA and UVB rays. I never put on sunscreen. Now parents slather sunscreen with high SPF all over their kids before the kids step out of the house. I'm not talking about when they're going to the beach. I'm talking about when they're walking to the car.

We also played with deadly poison on a regular basis. We called it bug spray.

We always kept a bug sprayer within reach, especially in summer. The sprayer had a wooden shaft with a bowl filled with pesticide attached underneath. It looked like an old-fashioned tommy gun. I treated it like a weapon, too. I would go outside, pretend I was a commando, and go on a search-and-destroy mission for bugs. If I saw a caterpillar or some other bug crawling around, I'd get right into its grille, say, "It's on," run inside, grab the bug sprayer, pump it like a shotgun, run back outside, and go all Rambo on its ass.

Everybody in our neighborhood grew vegetables, especially tomatoes. If we saw one bug crawling up the side of a tomato, it was *on*. I'd race into the garage, grab the tommy-gun bug sprayer, and douse the hell out of that tomato, which, of course, we would eat in a sandwich an hour later. We were convinced that the gnat or mosquito wandering around on the tomato carried the West Nile virus or dengue fever or some weird disease that turned you into a zombie. I took care of that. I pumped my tommy gun and drenched that tomato in a gallon of DEET or Off! By the time I was through, bug spray dripped down the sides of that tomato, forming a puddle on the ground. I wanted to make sure we were perfectly safe.

Then one summer about ten years ago I went up to Canada for a couple of club dates and stopped to play a round of golf in Winnipeg, which should be renamed Mosquitoville. Worst mosquitoes ever. Miniature dive-bombing insect terrorists. I wore jeans and it didn't matter. They bit right through my pants. Chewed holes through the denim. One of the pros at the club said, "Hey, man, use this," and he handed me a can of DDT. "Spray this on yourself. It's the only thing that works."

So I did. Rolled up my pants and doused my legs with the DDT.

Cracked the skin off. Left me with welts the color of Mars. I could barely walk. Killed the bugs, though.

I somehow made it to fifty by not flossing and by swallowing gallons of deadly bug spray. Now, I admit, I have started to obsess a little bit about my quality of life. If I end up with some nurse pushing me around in a wheelchair after she's just wiped my ass, I will seriously wheel myself off a cliff. So, I've been considering alternatives.

Cryogenics, for one thing.

Yes, freezing my body so I can come back to life in a hundred years.

Here's how it works: First, you do all the paperwork and make the arrangements with a special cryogenics company. You even have a choice of companies, because more and more people are going the cryogenics route. I heard that six hundred people have already been frozen, and now some celebrities have signed up, like Simon Cowell of *American Idol*, whom many people think couldn't get any colder, and Larry King—a surprise, because most people thought he died years ago, even when they watched him on TV.

After you fill out all the paperwork, you basically sit around and wait until you die. Or almost die. You can't *actually* die or you couldn't be frozen with any hope of coming back to life. You'd just be a human Popsicle. But you do have to *legally* die. Otherwise you'd be frozen alive. Bottom line: Once a doctor declares that there is nothing more he can do for you medically, the cryogenics people take over. They transfer you out of the hospital bed and drop you into a tank of liquid nitrogen at a nippy minus-238 degrees. They keep you in frozen storage for the next hundred years, or until you've instructed them to thaw you out.

I'm not sure about this.

For one thing, I heard there have been a few glitches with some of the cryogenics facilities. One place I read about had seventeen people frozen in tanks. Cost these people $200,000 for the procedure and for storage. A few years in, the company went bankrupt. They lost their lease, closed their business, and had to thaw everybody. That's not what they paid for. They didn't want to come back with this economy and no Oprah.

I'm confused, too, about the differences in price. Some companies charge $30,000 to be frozen, some way more, some way less. I'd be worried that somebody who's pissed at me would have me frozen according to my wishes, but they'd go with some shady cryonics company that would charge, like, $800 and shove my body into the freezer in the front of a 7-Eleven.

"Dude, get me a Coke, will ya?"

"Sure, man, let's see, a Coke— Whoa! That's George Lopez! You got G-Lo on ice!"

"Hey, grab your soda and close that thing, man. I gotta keep him in there for a hundred years. I had to do it so I could get lotto."

I don't know. This whole thing seems like a scam, like some fancy, frozen version of a storage unit.

Which is a sore subject with me.

I'm kicking myself now. Because if I listened to RJ back in the early eighties, I would've made a fortune. He wanted me to invest some money with this guy who came up with a brilliant, innovative idea.

Storage units.

Nobody had ever heard of this before.

"What the hell is that?" I said.

"Very simple," RJ said. "There's this building just off

the freeway, which he got cheap. He divided the building into small units, like closets, all different sizes. The idea is, you take everything out of your garage or your basement, all your crap, and you put it into one of these storage units."

"Into these closets by the freeway?"

"That's right."

I rolled my eyes. "Okay, yeah, and then what?"

"Then you get a key, so anytime you want to go over there and see your crap, you just go, open it up, and take a look."

"You drive over and open up your 'storage unit' so you can look at your crap?"

"Exactly."

"I'm not following this. What happens to all the crap in your garage?"

"It's not there anymore. You took it out. You put it in your storage unit."

"Which, I'm guessing, you paid for."

"Right."

"So, you've taken all your crap out of your garage and put it into a different place, and you've written a check—"

"Every month."

"Oh. You write a check every *month*."

"It's not that much. You pay, like, sixty bucks."

"Okay. And for sixty bucks a month, every month for as long as you live, you drive far from your house so you can visit your crap anytime you want."

"Now you got it."

I nodded. "I have one question: Who is gonna do

that? Who would want to drive somewhere else, near the goddamn freeway—for money—to see the stuff that you could've walked five feet to see in your garage for *free*?"

RJ paused. "It does sound messed-up."

"It *is* messed-up."

"The guy is gonna lose his shirt."

"He's an imbecile."

"He's an idiot," RJ said. "I wouldn't give him any money. I wouldn't give him a dime."

"Please."

We laughed like hell. Of course, I didn't invest any money in what turned out to be one of the biggest moneymaking ideas of the decade.

Then one day, in the early nineties, RJ rolled into my driveway behind the wheel of a brand-new Mercedes convertible. I ran my palm over the hood and sat down in the passenger seat. The ultrasoft leather squished expensively.

"Man, this is nice. Smells rich."

"You like it?"

"It's beautiful. How much you put down for this?"

"Nothing," RJ said. "I paid cash."

"You what? How can you afford that?"

"An investment I made a few years ago paid off. Did I ever tell you about it? Storage units. It's a dumb idea when you think about it—you know, putting your crap in a different place than your own garage and paying a monthly fee—but, hey, people are stupid. It's like printing money."

I don't blame RJ. It was my own fault. I couldn't pull

the trigger. I get that way sometimes when it comes to taking risks. That's probably why I won't have my body frozen. Too risky. I want to know what to expect when I thaw out. I need someone else to go first. I want a guy I know to come back and tell me how great it is before I commit. I wouldn't trust Simon Cowell. He'd be too critical. And I'm pretty sure Larry King died a few years ago.

I'm also afraid they'll mix me up with somebody else. I've checked the Internet. There are a lot of people with my name. Plus, it's happened to me before.

More than thirty years ago, when I was around twenty, I went on a bender one night and stupidly ended up getting a DUI. I landed in jail overnight. I'll never forget it: It was a Sunday night, and when I slept it off, I woke up Monday morning in a smelly, scary jail cell feeling horrible and embarrassed and disgusted with myself. I woke up lying on a metal bench. Every bone in my body ached. I forced myself to a sitting position and came eye-to-eye with a big dude, a heavyset Latino guy with huge blond hair flying all over, as if Gorgeous George had stuck his finger into a wall socket. He wore black eye makeup that had turned into blotches and spread all over his face, and he had bright orange lipstick smeared kind of near his mouth. I looked down and saw he had bare feet, and he had painted his toes orange to match his lipstick. He crossed his legs and wagged his knee, and I thought, "As if this could get any worse."

He smiled at me. I smiled back, and I thought, "I really hope this tranny doesn't kill me."

A few minutes later, a cop came over to our cell. He

looked down at a clipboard in his hand, squinted, and said, "Lopez?"

The heavyset dude with the big blond hair and the orange toes and I stood up at the same time. What were the odds? We were both named Lopez. We approached the cop.

"No," the cop said to me. "*Mrs.* Lopez."

The tranny winked at me.

My luck. If I agreed to do cryogenics, they would freeze the wrong Lopez. They'd take Tranny Lopez.

So, I've made my decision.

When I die, I do not want to be frozen.

Mainly because I'm not afraid of dying.

I came to peace with death by surviving kidney disease, turning fifty, and from my friend, golfing great Lee Trevino.

Lee didn't just look death in the face; he literally *died* and came back to life.

June 1975.

Lee and two other golfers walked onto a long par three at the Western Open at Butler National Golf Course in Oak Brook, Illinois, outside Chicago. Ominous silvery clouds had shadowed them all match. The clouds suddenly darkened, faded to pitch-black, and the winds kicked up. A crash of thunder jolted them and then the rains came. Some golfers, including Jack Nicklaus, scrambled off the fairway, sought shelter in the clubhouse and huts just off the course. Not Lee. He shrugged off the rain that pelted his shirt. He stood on the tee and squinted through the rain at the green a couple hundred yards away. The rain started coming down in sheets, slamming into the pond at the edge of the tee, not far from where Super Mex stood.

Lee bent over and stuck his ball and tee into the ground, stood up, and measured the distance from the tee to the green by extending his arm straight at the flag. He then pulled a one iron out of his bag, a tough club to hit, an unusual choice for this shot. But given the rain and wind, Lee knew that the one iron was the right choice, maybe even an inspired one. Few people struck a golf ball with the precision of Lee Trevino, and nobody hit with more swagger or more style. Lee took a practice swing and wiggled his shoulders as the rain slapped at his shirt and dribbled off the brim of his cap. He picked up his right foot and knocked off a clump of wet grass caught in his metal spikes.

Lee stepped up to his ball, swung, and smacked his drive through the pelting rain, now a torrent, jabbing the pond like a million needles. He locked his eyes on the flight of the ball, the one iron held straight up in perfect follow-through, aimed like a conqueror's sword. The ball arched toward the green, plopped onto the fringe, and rolled toward the cup, stopping a birdie length away. Thunder clapped. A flash of lightning zigzagged in front of him and spiderwebbed the pond.

Lee slowly lowered the one iron.

The lightning jumped the water and hopped across the grass, pulled by the attraction of a lightning rod. . . .

Lee's metal spikes.

*Broosh!*

The lightning smoked him, wrapping him in a cloak of fire and light.

Then the smell of something burning engulfed him, drifted into the air.

It smelled like someone was having a cookout, making carne asada.

And then far away, he heard the sound of footsteps squishing into the wet ground, followed by voices and screaming.

*"Lee!"*

He lay naked on the ground. The lightning had burned off his clothes. Towels flew through the rain, finding him, covering him.

More screaming, running, panic.

"I heard everything," Lee told me. "I didn't know the lightning burned off my clothes, but I heard all the commotion and then I heard somebody say, 'He's dead.'"

"You heard that?" I said.

"Yes. And then I felt myself being lifted. I started going up, up into the air above the golf course. Floating. Hovering. I was above the whole thing. Then I looked down and I saw myself. That's when I realized I was dead."

"Unbelievable. You actually died."

"Yes. And then I saw that light. It was exactly what people talk about. But it's warm. Soothing. It *bathes* you. You feel very warm and comfortable and calm. Then I saw my mother. And I saw my grandmother. I saw my whole family, everybody who died. Then all of a sudden I heard a voice coming from far away, like from down a hallway. *'Lee, Lee.'* The voice got stronger and stronger, and I saw my family standing there and I wanted to go to them. I tried to go to them, but the voice calling my name got louder and I turned toward it and the faces of my family got dimmer and then they all faded out."

"What about the light?"

"It went out. It sort of clicked off. And then I woke up and I was on the ground, people all around me. Then I realized I was alive, but I had died. My back hurt like hell, and I was thankful to be alive, and from now on I'll think twice about hitting a one iron."

He paused.

"But, you know, when it's time for me to go, I'm not afraid anymore, because I already know what it's like. I've been there. I know it's not horrible."

So, thanks to Lee Trevino, I'm not afraid of dying. And after Lee told me about seeing that light, I heard it from other people, too. A guitar player who played in the band on my show had the same experience. He had a terrible accident; he died, saw the light, and came back.

When you hit fifty, you do think about the end. It all feels as if it's coming at you a little too fast. Maybe that's because it is. There are more days behind you than ahead of you. It's that simple. But when the end comes, I'm ready. Or as ready anybody can be.

I hope I'm not hit by lightning, though. I don't want to be smoked and barbecued. Especially in public. I'm gonna try to stay out of storms. I'm sure as hell not running to lightning. It's bad enough that I have to see myself with no clothes on.

# THE LAST DAYS OF CREEPY LITTLE WHITE GIRL

**AND** now a word about the executive at TBS who canceled my talk show, *Lopez Tonight,* less than two years after it began, and gave me, my staff, my crew, and my band thirty-six hours to get out of the building.

Fuck that *puto.*

I know. That's not right.

That's three words.

Do I seem bitter?

I'm not.

I gave up being bitter, angry, vengeful, and feeling stabbed in the back when I turned fifty.

I still might feel a little pissed off. . . .

Hey, at least I'm not lying.

In 2004, a dear friend, Jim Paratore, a top television executive, asked if he could meet with me.

"You ever consider doing a talk show?" Jim asked me.

"Thanks, Jim, but I got a job," I said. At the time, I was working day and night on *The George Lopez Show,* which was still going strong on ABC. I also had kidney disease and was fighting for my life. I felt kind of overextended.

"Your sitcom won't run forever," Jim said. "Think about it."

"I will."

Two years later, we shot our one hundredth *George Lopez Show* episode. By the end of that season, the sitcom's run on the network came to an end. Jim didn't waste much time. He called me a few weeks later and again pitched me a late-night talk show.

Jim was passionate and convincing. The more he sold me, the more he won me over. I started to embrace the idea. "If I do a late-night show, I want to use *Arsenio* as a template," I said. "I want to do a show that you can't see on TV right now. I want the show to be diverse and inclusive and edgy."

"So do we," Jim said.

"I want the show to be a reflection of me," I said.

"Us, too," Jim said.

With Jim as our champion, we put together a top-notch staff and crew and added the unbelievable Michael Bearden to lead our kick-ass band. Sadly, Jim recently passed away. I'll always be grateful for his support. He was one of the truly good guys.

*Lopez Tonight* debuted November 9, 2009. My first guests were Eva Longoria, Ellen DeGeneres, and my friends Carlos Santana and Kobe Bryant. That night our ratings blew the roof off. We beat everybody—Leno, Letterman, Kimmel, Conan, and Jon Stewart. We beat 'em all.

Of course, we couldn't keep it up. We strove to keep the show honest and fun and diverse as we struggled to maintain solid ratings. Creatively, we wrote sketches and introduced segments that definitely went outside the box. Way outside, like the popular "Creepy Little White Girl," featuring a little kid holding a headless doll and singing "Ring Around the Rosie" before she gave me terrible news. Some sketches worked, some didn't, but we kept trying to push the envelope. All new shows suffer growing pains, and we experienced our share. We adjusted. We brought in a new executive producer who had worked with David Letterman. We knew that in order for us to succeed, everyone had to commit to the long term. Talk shows are a grind, and most experts agree that it takes at least three years to find your groove. Some say you need a minimum of five years.

I never worked harder. Some nights after doing the show I would walk into my house, have a few bites of dinner, and literally collapse. I loved the show, loved the people I worked with, felt proud of what we were doing. But sometimes I wondered if this grueling schedule was worth it. I would ask myself, "Am I doing the right thing? Is this what I should be doing, spending my career talking about other people's careers?"

Every so often something would happen that would energize me and validate all our hard work. That first year our bookers scored a major showbiz coup. They booked Prince, who never does talk shows and rarely does TV. When he sat down next to me on the set and the audience frenzy died down, I said to him, "I have one question. Why? Why choose me?"

Prince said, "I find this show represents all people. I see all kinds of guests on here." The audience erupted in applause, and while the cheering nearly drowned him out, he added, "I'm on this show because you're kind to everyone."

That moment gave me chills. Prince made me feel that we were offering viewers a real alternative, and that on this night, at least, we were doing something special.

By then, TBS had assigned a new executive to our show, a guy I'll call Mel after Mel Cooley from the old *Dick Van Dyke Show*. I thought I'd start hearing from Mel pretty regularly after the show with Prince, because with that show I felt we'd turned a corner.

No.

Didn't hear from him.

Silence.

Then, in early 2010, the late-night talk-show world exploded.

NBC's experiment of moving Jay Leno to ten o'clock, five nights a week, while handing over *The Tonight Show* to Conan O'Brien, had turned into a ratings disaster. Basically, America—yes, the entire country—decided not to watch either of them. Trying to correct this mistake, NBC handed *The Tonight Show* back to Leno and bought out Conan—for $40 million. TBS immediately swarmed in and went after Conan to do a late-night show. I pictured Mel in intense closed-door meetings selling Conan, as if Mel were a used-car salesman. What I didn't expect was the closed-door meeting Mel had with me.

"I have a chance to get Conan," he said. "It's a track meet, and we have to beat somebody else to the finish line. We're gonna win. We want Conan bad."

"Great, okay, good luck with it," I said. "And what does this have to do with me?"

"We want you to slide to midnight," Mel said. "We're going to put Conan on at eleven."

"My time slot."

"Yes. But it's all good. We'll promote you as a block, you and Conan together. The new faces of late night. It's win-win."

"When would this happen?"

"November."

"November," I repeated. "Our show will be less than a year old."

"Correct," Mel said. "So what do you think?"

Even though I hesitated for probably less than five seconds, I felt that time had stopped. I thought, "Should I do this? Should I slide over? Do I really need this? Should I say no? But you know what? You're a team player. It's the nice thing to do. It's the right thing to do. Yes. You should do it."

"I'll do it," I said to Mel.

I never should've done it.

I know the old saying that hindsight is twenty-twenty, but I believe moving *Lopez Tonight* to midnight did us in. But I tried to please everybody. I wanted to be Mr. Nice Guy, the good soldier, the team player.

I should've listened to what my idol, Bill Cosby, said years ago. I look up to him more than anybody. Cos said, "I can't tell you the formula for success. But I can tell you that the formula for failure is trying to make everybody happy."

That was my problem. I tried to make everybody happy.

It turned out that I didn't make anybody happy, including me.

After TBS announced that they signed Conan for a billion dollars, or whatever they gave him on top of his $40 million buyout from NBC, I brought on Chris Rock as a guest. We caught up with each other on the air for a minute or so, and then I said, "You heard that Conan's coming to TBS?"

Chris said, "Conan's coming?"

"Yes."

"Where you going?"

"I'm staying," I said. "I'm going to midnight. He's coming on at eleven o'clock."

"Get the hell outta here."

"It's true."

"So you gonna move for the white man, huh? I hope he appreciates that."

"I think he does," I said quietly.

"And you don't have to clean or park nothing?"

"No," I said. "And here's the best part: I get to go to work an hour later. It's a Latino's dream, man."

The studio audience roared and Chris cracked up and I felt pretty good. At that moment, I was convinced that Conan and I would form an edgy, fresh, powerful two-hour block of late-night entertainment that the network would nurture and promote the hell out of.

I was wrong.

I drank the Kool-Aid.

TBS did promote the hell out of Conan. They just lost sight of me. Or they lost faith in the show. Or they thought that we had too much "flavor" for the time slot. Or the "flavor" of our show caused the Conan audience to drop off. Or—

I really don't know.

I do know that TBS canceled *Lopez Tonight* less than two years after we started.

When the media reported the show was canceled, the Reverend Jesse Jackson himself stepped in and tried to save it. He called Mel at TBS directly, and said television needed more diversity, and without us there would be a void. But TBS shot him down, too.

Mel never broke the news to me directly. He never called me. He told my agents the news. I got an e-mail. Mel also informed us that we had thirty-six hours to vacate the building. All of a sudden he became the Creepy Little White Girl.

Man, talk about night and day.

Conan got $40 million to leave NBC and I got thirty-six hours to get out of town.

I took the high road. I wanted our last show to be a party, and it was. I invited a few friends, Slash, and some other rockers, and I booked Derek Fisher and Metta World Peace (then Ron Artest) from my beloved Los Angeles Lakers, and Eva Longoria, who appeared on my first show. In the monologue I joked about being unemployed.

"Now that I lost my job, people want to know what I'm gonna do next. Well, like every other unemployed TV star, I'm gonna find me some crack. Yes. I'm going on the pipe. I'm gonna lose that unwanted hundred and ten pounds."

Everybody laughed and applauded, and at the end of the show the band played "Rock and Roll All Nite," and everybody stood up and danced.

We had a party, man.

It's all good.

But late night lost a little flavor.

# THINGS YOU SHOULD DO BEFORE YOU DIE, I MEAN, TURN FIFTY

**WHEN** I turned fifty, I decided not to think about the future. I mean, what if I didn't *have* a future? The future is *now*, man. I live in the moment. I try to be as present as I can. I don't like to plan and I hate to anticipate. That's why, when I came across this Web site that asked people over fifty what they would like to accomplish now that they've reached this milestone—things that they'd never done but that they finally might be willing to try because it's pretty much now or never—I thought, "You know what? I'm pretty adventurous. I'm game. Let's try some of this. Bring it on."

So, here we go.

Here's the first thing I found on that Web site list that people wanted to do. The first adventure.

"Ride something bigger than a horse."

Okay, let's think about this.

For starters, I paid a fortune for these teeth. My luck, I'll get up on a bull or an elephant, the thing will buck and throw me, and I'll swallow one of my veneers. I am not losing those $100,000 Chiclets. I'll have a surgeon go in after it, cut me open, and pull my veneers out. I'll wash it off and pop it back on. Those teeth are expensive, man. Plus they look good.

So, what would I ride?

Got it.

I'd ride a camel.

I would.

At least I think I would.

Camels can be nasty. They spit and they sweat and they smell like shit. They also have a lot of dander, and I'm violently allergic to dander. I know I'll inhale that camel dander and start sneezing and coughing and throw my back out. I can't handle camel dander. I know that sounds made-up, but it's not. That dander wrecks me. If I have to, I'll get a doctor's note. You know, like the kid who brings a note to school that says he can't get anywhere near peanuts. I can't get anywhere near camel dander.

But there's actually something else about riding a camel that makes me even more nervous. There is something I dread.

What if I didn't fit in between the humps?

That would get to me.

Okay, I may not look fat to you—and I may not actually *be* fat—but I am fat in my mind. Seriously. I'm fat.

So, yes, the worst thing would be if I approached the camel and the camel wrangler looked me over and said, "I'm sorry. This camel won't work. Can you come back Thursday? We have a camel in Phoenix that I think would fit you."

That would crush me.

If the camel wrangler informed me, "We don't have a

camel on hand that's your size, but we can special-order one for you. An extra-large. You don't want the space between the humps to be too snug. You want some room to breathe. A too-tight fit can be extremely uncomfortable. Jostle your balls. Cause some permanent damage. You might upset the camel, too. You do not want that. So should I put through the special order?"

Yes, that's my fear: that I would be too large for the camel.

I'm also a little concerned about getting up on a camel. My first thought was that I would need a ladder, but I'm too old for that. I don't want to be halfway up the camel, he turns around, smells me, makes a face, and bolts, leaving me in midair holding on to the ladder like I'm Francois the Clown in the Cirque du freaking Soleil.

I know that most professional camel riders and people living in the desert who ride camels all the time don't use a ladder. They mount by getting the camel to sit on the ground. They make a clicking sound; then they say, "Jit, jit, jit"—which is how some Mexicans pronounce the word "shit," so I know I can handle that—over and over, until the camel bends his knees and slowly lowers himself onto the ground.

This sounds great, except that after the age of fifty, your range of motion starts to go. When I was a kid, I used to climb trees and hop fences, no problem. I was as athletic as anyone. I even learned to climb the rope at school. Everyone hated climbing the rope. I did, too, at first. But I was determined to conquer it. Took me weeks. Every day in gym class, I worked my way up the rope a little more, then a little more, literally inch by inch, until I got all the way to the ceiling. I remember that feeling of triumph and accomplishment. What a rush! I felt like a fireman. Then I realized I had to get down. I hadn't factored that in. I came down, shinnying hand over hand, but I went too fast. I burned the hell out of my palms. I walked around with salve on my hands for a week. I smelled like an old person's ass.

**TO TELL YOU THE TRUTH, I'M NOT SURE I'D BE ABLE TO CLIMB ONTO A CAMEL EVEN IF THE CAMEL WAS SITTING ON THE GROUND.**

To tell you the truth, I'm not sure I'd be able to climb onto a camel even if the camel was sitting on the ground. I think I'd need a hoist. Or I'd have to wear a harness and have some kind of pulley lift me up, move me over, and drop me down onto the camel in between the camel's humps, assuming I fit. And then once we got going and I was up and riding, what if the camel didn't listen when I said, "Jit, jit, jit," and the fool wouldn't sit down? What if he got pissed and went ballistic and reared up and threw me and got dander all over me and I got an allergic reaction and I started sneezing uncontrollably and my back went out?

You know what?

I'm not riding on a camel.

What's next on the list?

"Spend twenty-four hours alone in the jungle."

Yes. Absolutely.

This would be an interesting challenge, because I'm from the city. I'm normally not a fan of wildlife or big game or rashes. I'm not a fan of smaller game, either. I've never held a frog or a lizard and I never want to. Those things creep me out. And ever since I heard that rumor about Richard Gere years ago, I won't get anywhere near a gerbil or any kind of furry little rodent. There are also a lot of snakes in the jungle, and I hate snakes. They scare the crap out of me. I also don't like strange-looking plants, even if they're full of beautiful flowers. I'm sure the one flower I touched would either be filled with poison or be the one plant in the world that had teeth.

Maybe instead of staying overnight in the jungle, I'd consider spending a night in MacArthur Park in L.A. Actually, that's more dangerous than the jungle. I'd get killed in that park. No lie. I don't know what's going on in there, but I know it's bad. For one thing, you never see anybody walking in L.A. So if something terrible happened to me in the park and I tried to run out for help, I know that there would be nobody around. It's unbelievable. How is it possible that in a city with a population of more than three million you never see any people? Where the hell are they? And all the cars have tinted windows, so you still don't see anybody. The only people you see are walking their dogs. Those people are really dangerous. You can't approach them, because they all carry Mace or some shit, especially near MacArthur Park. So, no, I'm not spending twenty-four hours in the park, because I don't want some crazy person to spray me in the face with something that I'd be allergic to and then I'd start sneezing uncontrollably and throw my back out.

Actually, wait a minute; I did see one person walking on the street.

My neighbor.

He walks all the time.

He's an older guy, my age, maybe even sixty.

He's in pretty good shape. You can tell because he walks with shorts, no shirt.

But he's old-school.

He reads a book while he walks.

Not an audiobook. He doesn't have a headset. He holds an actual book. A *book* book. With a cover and a binding and pages and everything.

The guy's a dinosaur.

He walks and reads. Pretty fast pace, too. Head down, eyes focused on the page, never looking up, walking and reading, reading and walking.

This guy is gonna get killed.

Cars whiz by him. He doesn't notice.

Someday a guy driving a car is gonna see this guy walking and reading, and the driver is gonna say, "What is that guy doing? What is that in his hand? What *is* that?" And he's gonna lose control of the car and jump the curb and run him over.

Death by reading.

I guess it's not a bad way to go.

Next.

"Set foot on each of the seven continents."

Okay, this I can do.

Let's see.

I live in North America, so that's one.

I've been to Europe.

Two.

Then there's South America, Asia, Africa, Australia, and Antarctica.

You know what?

I don't have time.

I'm too old.

By the time I set foot in the other five, I'll be seventy-five, easy. I can't plan for something that far off. This one shouldn't be for people over fifty. This is a goal for somebody in his twenties. It's like a lifetime achievement goal.

Actually, I can cross off Antarctica, because growing up in L.A., I've already been there.

I grew up in a tract house with no air-conditioning and no heater. The summers were never the problem, because the days were warm and bearable. We would have what everyone called a dry heat, but with a breeze, and at night the temperature dropped. I slept with the windows open to allow the cool air in. There were only a couple of weeks a year, usually in September, when the temperature rose and the heat hit you so hard that you couldn't move and your clothes stuck to you.

Winter, though, was brutal.

Maybe it was how our house was built, but once winter came and the temperature at night fell into the forties, the walls seemed to lock the cool air in tight with no escape. Our tract house became an igloo. Some nights it got so cold that I'd get into bed and run in place. I'd pull the blankets up to my chin and kick like I was treading water, trying to warm up the one spot that I confined myself to. Sometimes I could see my breath in my bedroom. I'd go, "Huh," and blow out air on purpose so I could watch a cloud form from my breath. I thought, "Damn, this is crazy. I'm in my bedroom, lying in bed—in *Los Angeles*—and I can see my breath as if I was outside in North Buttrash, Alaska."

Once I got the bed nice and warm in my one spot, I'd lie there without moving, like a corpse. Because if I accidentally rolled over in the middle of the night and hit a part of the bed that I hadn't warmed up, it felt like I'd rolled over onto a freezer door. I'm telling you, this room was *cold*.

So, as far as I'm concerned, yes, I've already experienced Antarctica, every night during every winter I lived in that house.

I should've put a flag in the middle of my room, like an explorer sticking a flag in the middle of an ice cap.

Okay, let's see what else these people wanted to do after fifty.

"Cross the country on a bicycle."

Oh, this is a must. Positively.

One hitch.

Not sure I can make it across the whole country. In fact, my ass couldn't take fifteen minutes on a bike seat. I know, because I bought some workout equipment and it sits in my house pretty much unused. I did buy a stationary bike. I tried to ride that thing. I set it up in front of the TV. I know you're not supposed to do that. Some guy at the gym I used to belong to, a trainer, I guess, told me that watching TV while you exercise distracts you from focusing on the exercise you're doing. Your mind and your body should be concentrating on the same thing at the same time. The hell with that. If I don't watch TV, I'm not doing exercise. I *want* to be distracted. To me, that's the point.

And once you get out on the road, you're taking your life in your hands. I don't want to be pedaling my ass off on my bike and all of a sudden I get blindsided by some kid driving a car texting his girlfriend asking her, "Hey, where you wanna eat and what are you wearing?"

It's bad enough that after you turn fifty, your body starts to fall apart all on its own. I don't think you should give it any help. You don't need to stress it out.

I seriously don't want to tempt fate. I don't ski, I don't run, and I don't ride a bike outdoors, because these activities are just too dangerous. I know a guy in his fifties who ran all the time. Great shape. One night he decided to go for a run. He stretched, because he didn't want to pull anything. Then he set his watch and began running. He hit the street, picked up speed, turned a corner, stepped in a hole, flew up in the air, landed on his head, crushed his skull, broke his cheekbone, snapped his collarbone, and tore up his knee. Somehow the dude lived, even though he went in, like, seven different directions at once. Forget it. Do your workout indoors.

Next.

"Run a marathon."

Bingo. I actually have some experience with this.

I took up running right after I turned fifty.

Well, briefly.

In fact, I ran a 5K race with my buddy RJ.

RJ had been married for about a year, and like all newlywed husbands, he'd ballooned up. Put on a good forty pounds. I'm not sure why newlyweds always gain weight, but they all do. I did. It's automatic: You get married and a year later you're forty pounds heavier. And it's not just men. Women, too. It could be that you're giving off a different vibe, a married person's vibe, an unconscious signal to the world that announces, "Hey, everybody, I'm out of action."

As soon as you make that unconscious announcement, you give yourself permission to let go. You no longer feel pressure that you have to keep in perfect shape or stay trim. You're done. Off the market. You have scored. No more sad and lonely nights. No more singles scenes. Say good-bye to barhopping, clubbing, and, best of all, your friends' horrible fix-ups. You're married now, and you're content (that's the key word: *content*) to chill out at home, watch some TV, and . . . eat.

I remember when my ex-wife and I had that first conversation about staying in. It was in the fall of 1993. The world was a different place then. We were speaking to each other.

"You know what?" my newly beloved said. "Let's not go out. Let's have dinner together here, just the two of us. Let's have steak. You run the barbecue."

"Sounds great," I lied.

"We'll have a nice quiet dinner and then snuggle and watch *Beverly Hills 90210* and *Melrose Place*," my wife said.

"I love that idea," I lied again.

Back then, before I was fifty, I lied all the time. It was much easier. Way less hassle. Why tell her that the last thing I wanted to do was watch *Beverly Hills 90210* and *Melrose Place*? I didn't want to waste an evening doing something meaningless. I wanted to do something productive, like polish my golf tees.

And why admit that I didn't know the first thing about barbecuing? What would've been the point?

I had to start from scratch. We didn't own any cookbooks, and I had never seen a cooking show. Nobody had. This was 1993, at least ten years before the Food Network started. Nobody could imagine that chefs showing you how to cook would become hot TV shows. I never would've thought that somebody could actually be a "celebrity chef." That would have been an oxymoron, like "reality TV actor" or "moderate Republican."

I racked my brain for a clue on how to barbecue. We didn't do much grilling or barbecuing in my neighborhood, but I remembered a dish I used to love at Gladstones on the beach that they cooked over an open fire.

"Steaks aren't enough," I said to my wife. "We need a side dish. I know what I'm gonna do. Be right back."

I ran out to the market and got us some shrimp. I came home, fired up the grill, put on a couple of thick steaks, and then dumped the shrimp into a pouch I made out of aluminum foil, just like I'd seen at Gladstones. I seasoned the shrimp with salt, pepper, and a dash of chili flakes, dropped in an entire stick of butter, nudged the steaks over to make room, put the aluminum pouch on the grill, and turned up the heat.

*Zzzzp.*

Oh, man, those shrimp sizzled.

My mouth watered as I stood over the grill and poked the steak and shrimp with my metal spatula and tongs. I thought, "Wow, I have a talent for barbecuing. It's a gift."

"Smells great," my wife said.

"I know," I said. "But one side dish isn't enough."

I grabbed a fresh loaf of sourdough bread, sliced up the whole thing, buttered every slice, and lightly grilled each one.

As we settled in to watch *Beverly Hills 90210*, I plated our dinners—steak, shrimp grilled in butter, grilled buttered bread, and several beers.

Delicious.

We ate this way pretty much every night.

When I weighed myself at the end of that first year of marriage, I was shocked that I'd gained forty pounds.

I thought I'd gained at least sixty. I felt relieved, for about two seconds. Then I felt fat. Bloated. Enormous. And disgusted that I'd let myself balloon up like this.

I stood on the scale staring as my weight settled into that plus-forty column. I got off the scale and stepped back on to be sure. Yes. Still plus forty.

My wife came up behind me and looked over my shoulder. "We have to lose weight," she said.

"We?"

"Well, you."

I don't know why, but after a year of marriage, I wanted a little less "we" and a little more "me."

Actually, I wanted less of "me," too. I wanted to get back into shape

Of course, I saw this coming. I knew I was gaining weight because my pants didn't fit.

For me, not being able to fit into my favorite jeans was a huge wake-up call. That and stepping onto the scale and then looking into the mirror and seeing this fat Mexican guy. All the proof I needed. I'd gained a ton of weight and I knew it.

I'm amazed that some dudes can't see themselves and how much weight they've gained. It should be obvious. If you look in the mirror and see your stomach bulging out of your shirt, the flab flopping over your pants, hanging out there, jiggling like a giant tub of Jell-O, doesn't it set off, like, a million warning bells? It has to register. You have to say to yourself, "Whoa, I am putting on weight. Look at that. I'm borderline *fat*."

You can't deny it. It's right in front of you. Literally.

Listen, I worry about my weight every day, especially since I turned fifty. I take any weight gain seriously.

In fact, I have my own way of gauging my weight before I even look in the mirror or step on the scale.

I call it the Belly Button Test.

I take this test the moment I wake up.

First, I take the setup to the test. All I do is lie on my side and rub my stomach. If my stomach feels bigger than I remember from the night before, I panic. Most of the time, I'm okay. I rub my gut and I say, "All right, that feels good. I'm okay."

Now, if you can't get over onto your side, go ahead and panic. You already failed the test, because, seriously, you're already way too fat to even take the too-fat test.

But, okay, let's say I'm not too freaked out about my stomach. Then I do the Belly Button Test.

Here's what I do.

Very simple.

I push my belly button in and see how deep it goes.

That's my barometer. It works all the time.

It's the same idea as those boats that have a stick in the back (called a Power-Pole or a spike) that's used to determine the depth of the water. As the boat approaches the dock, you can see the most recent waterline on the stick. If the stick's soaked all the way to the top, you know that the boat's been safe, that it hasn't gotten too close to shore. You do not want your boat to go all the way in. The stick is your warning. If the boat stick has no waterline, that means you've literally hit bottom. You do not want to hit bottom. That's trouble. That means your boat is about to crash.

My belly button is my stick.

Only I do it in reverse.

How far I push it in tells me how fat I am.

If I push in my belly button and my hand keeps going, disappearing into my flesh all the way up to my wrist, that's a warning sign. That signifies that I've put on way too much weight. That indicates that I'm a whale.

The Belly Button Test is very scientific.

Because it's real.

You have to keep it real when it comes to your weight, because you will lie to yourself. Your mind will play tricks on you.

I always lied to myself when I shopped for pants. I shopped for pants a lot, because I had to. I would go up and down constantly. I went in and out of more weight classes than Oprah.

When you fluctuate like that, it's not just the physical act of gaining weight that gets to you. It's the psychological part of it that really does you in. It's amazing how deeply my weight is tied to my emotions. When I lost weight, I'd be thrilled. But if I got on the scale and I'd gained?

I felt devastated, depressed, worthless, and like I had all this hard work ahead of me. It was demoralizing.

So, the easiest way to deal with it was to lie.

Especially when I would shop for pants.

Before I even hit the men's department, I was prepared. I carried a number in my head, a number I would say when the salesperson asked, "Would you like to try on some pants? Shall I get you a fitting room?"

"Please."

"And what is your size?"

"Thirty-four."

I said this with a straight face.

"Thirty-*four*?"

"Yes."

"And what about the other leg?"

That's what I expected him to say.

But all he did was put his hand on his waist and tilt his head and stare me down.

I stared right back. I didn't flinch.

Finally I caved.

"You know what? I just remembered. I left my sunglasses in the car. I'll be right back."

I didn't come back.

Until I lost the weight.

A few months after I turned fifty, I went shopping for pants in a well-known department store. I'd been experiencing some violent weight fluctuation, and again I put that wishful number in my head: thirty-four.

But this time, the salesclerk who approached me was a young, extremely attractive woman.

"I'm Brianna," she said in a throaty voice. She smiled. Her eyes were gray-green, smoky, and sexy. I could see myself drowning in them. "May I help you?" she purred.

"I need some jeans," I said.

Brianna looked me up and down. She undressed me with her eyes. "I know what would look really good on you," she said.

I followed her to a rack of jeans in the back corner of the men's department. She flicked through a bunch of jeans and stopped at a particular style and cut. "Try these on," Brianna said. "These are hot."

The moment she opened her mouth and the word "hot" danced out on the tip of her delicious-looking tongue, my mouth got dry as Bakersfield. I took a step and started to lose my balance. I felt light-headed. I thought I was going to fall over.

And then, suddenly, my mind left my body.

I was no longer in the men's department of that store.

Brianna and I were together, a happy couple, walking hand in hand. We were sitting across from each other in a restaurant, having brunch, sipping mimosas. We entwined our arms, clinked glasses, sipped, and laughed.

Then we were driving up the coast in my convertible, the waves crashing below us, her head thrown back, her hair blowing in the wind.

Then we were slow-dancing on the beach to soft violin music and the crackle of a bonfire, the shadows of the flames licking our backs.

And then we were lying in bed entangled in satin sheets, a circle of lit candles and incense burning all around us. Suddenly she turned her naked body toward mine, opened her mouth to kiss me, and said—

"What size is your waist?"

"Huh?"

I blinked and found myself standing in the men's department again, across from Brianna. She held two pairs of jeans draped across her arms. "The jeans," she said.

"Yes?"

"What size?"

"Thirty-four," I squeaked.

She coughed. She cleared her throat. "That's what I thought," she said.

She stuck her hand into some more jeans hanging from the rack, pulled out another pair, and placed that on top of the other two. "Would you like to try these on?"

"I would, yes, definitely, absolutely."

"Right this way."

I followed her into the dressing room area. She found a vacant room, pushed the saloon door open, and put my jeans on the bench against the far wall.

"Let me know how these fit," she said, and winked.

"I will, thanks," I said.

She winked again, left the dressing room, and closed the door behind her.

"Thirty-four," I said softly, as I pulled off my old jeans and grabbed one of the jeans from the bench. "Come on, thirty-*four*."

The second I pulled the jeans past my knees I knew they were never gonna fit. I pulled harder. "Fit, you hot jeans," I said. *"Fit."*

> **I SUCKED IN MY GUT AS FAR AS I COULD AND YANKED THE BUTTON TOWARD THE BUTTONHOLE. "YOU CAN DO IT. COME ON!"**

I sucked in my gut as far as I could and yanked the button toward the buttonhole. "You can do it. Come on!"

I sucked my gut in even more and pulled both sides of the jeans with all my might. I gritted my teeth. I puffed out my cheeks. I inhaled and exhaled and grunted like I was a weight lifter.

I couldn't get the jeans on. But I refused to give up. "You are gonna do this," I said.

I swept the other jeans off the bench and lay down on it. I drew in my stomach and brought the button toward the buttonhole. I woofed. I groaned. I moaned. The button sneaked closer to the buttonhole. Closer. Closer. *I'm gonna do this.* Two inches away. An inch and a half. An inch—

I lost my grip. The waist of the pants flew out of my hands. "Son of a *bitch!*"

"Are you all right in there?"

Brianna.

I sat up on the bench. "Yes! I'm fine. I love these jeans so much, I lost control. 'Son of a bitch, are these jeans hot!' That's what I said."

"I told you," her voice sang over the saloon door of the dressing room.

"Yes, you did. You were right," I said. "I'm gonna try on another pair."

"Great. I'll be right out here."

I edged back down on the bench and wriggled out of the jeans. I picked up another pair. "What am I gonna do?" I said. "These are never gonna fit."

I sighed, and then something on the label caught my eye.

A number.

*Thirty-six.*

"Nice," I said.

Brianna had slipped me a thirty-six when I wasn't looking. She didn't believe I could fit into a thirty-four. She knew that was the number I had in my head, the number I came in with, my wish number. And then it hit me.

Hot, sexy Brianna with the smoky eyes really liked me.

It all came rushing back, and there I was in that slow-motion romantic-comedy montage that usually stars

Jennifer Lopez and some hot guy in his twenties. But instead of J-Lo it was me and Brianna. Brunch. Mimosas. Driving up the coast. Slow-dancing on the bench. Satin sheets and incense.

Trash that thirty-four.

Give me that thirty-six and let's get them on and get *it* on.

I lay back down on the bench and wriggled the thirty-sixes up my legs, past my knees, up to my waist, lifted my butt, and—

They didn't fit.

The stupid jeans did not fit.

"No," I said.

I inhaled and pulled the waist of the jeans up, with everything I had.

The thirty-sixes did not *fit*.

"No," I repeated. "No! *Noooo!*"

I started to cry.

I was too fat to fit into the thirty-sixes.

What was I supposed to do now, ask Brianna for a *thirty-eight*?

"How are those?"

Brianna again.

But there was something about her voice now.

She sounded different. She'd gone all cold and businesslike. She no longer sounded like my sexy soul mate. She sounded like a salesclerk trying to sell me a pair of pants.

I sniffed. "They're, you know, good, real good, little snug—"

"Snug?"

It was over.

What was I supposed to say?

"Yes, Brianna, those thirty-sixes are too tight. Bring me a forty, will you? And throw in a forty-two for insurance, too, will you?"

That's not going to work.

How's this?

"Hey, Brianna, you know what? I'm gonna forget pants for today. They're too tight. I'm just gonna starve myself and use laxatives every hour until I drop the weight. I'll be back in three weeks. I will fit into those thirty-fours and you and I will be tooling up the coast."

"Are you okay in there?"

She was just outside the dressing room door, but she sounded a million miles away.

"Yeah. I'm fine."

"Sounds like you're crying."

"Yeah, yeah, no, I love these pants so much. I get very emotional when I try on a wonderful pair of jeans. I get overcome. But you know what? I remembered I left my sunglasses in the car and I'm just gonna run down to the garage—"

"I can ring these up for you so when you get back—"

"That's okay, no, thanks, but I'll be right back. I'll come right back."

"Whatever."

I heard her high heels clacking out of the dressing room area and out of my life.

"Yeah, whatever," I said.

I stood up, pulled on my old pair of jeans, and looked at myself in the mirror.

Which was when that day got even worse.

Looking in the mirror I saw *It*.

The one thing I'd been dreading I'd see when I turned fifty. I knew it was a matter of time.

"No," I said. "It can't be. Not here. Not now."

But there it was, plain as day, glaring at me from the back of my hand.

A liver spot.

My first one.

The little brown dot just showed up. Just like that.

I suppose I was glad that it appeared on my hand and not on my forehead or on my nose.

I had a plan for this, too.

Before I left the house, I would put some M&M's on the back of my hand and let them melt. Then if somebody saw my liver spot and said, "Hey, whoa, what is that? Is that a . . . liver spot?"

"No, man, that's just some chocolate." And I'd start licking it off.

No way I was accepting a liver spot.

I jammed my hand into my pocket, walked out of the dressing room, and got the hell out of that department store.

After that humiliating afternoon in the men's department, I went to work. I cut back on my calorie intake and started to eat a lot of salads. I also started walking the stairs inside my house. I knew it wasn't enough. I had to do more. But what?

One afternoon I got a call from RJ. "I'm running a marathon," he said.

"You're what?"

"I'm running a marathon. Twenty-six miles, consecutively, all at once."

"I know what it is. And I heard you the first time. I just wanted to hear you say it again, because it sounds so funny."

"That's not the funny part. Here's the funny part. You're gonna run it with me."

"You're right. That is funny. That's hilarious. I don't run. I hate to run; you know that."

"You have to."

"Really? And why is that?"

"Because if I can do it, you can do it."

"That's not a good reason, RJ. That's a terrible reason."

"How's this? You got heavy."

He had me there.

I really didn't want to run—I do hate running—but I thought that maybe in this case it might be worth it. And since I'd crossed off everything else on that "things to do when you turn fifty" bucket list, I thought maybe I should try at least one thing.

"You know what? I'm gonna do it."

"All right! I'm holding you to it. We begin training tomorrow."

"Training?"

"Yes. This is serious. You won't regret this."

"I regret it already."

I went to the Nike store that afternoon and decked

myself out with some cool running clothes. As long as I was gonna run outside, where people could see me, I had to make sure I looked good. Because you never know. Somebody might see me and get interested in something more physical and fun than running.

I bought some cushy, expensive cross-trainers, some very hip T-shirts, a pack of sweatbands, knee pads, and some salve to rub on my nipples in case they chafed. Hey, that's what I heard. You run too hard in the heat, your nipples get sore, crack, and chafe. I couldn't imagine anything much worse than a couple of chafed nipples. I wanted to avoid that. Not taking any chances. I also took a peek around the store and behind the counter to see if they sold dick-chafing cream. I figured if your nipples chafe, your dick might, too.

I also bought several pairs of flashy running shorts. The great thing about these was the elastic waistband. After my horrifying jeans-buying experience, I loved the idea of pants with a waistband that stretched. One size fit all. I didn't want to worry about whether my running shorts were gonna be too big or, God forbid, too snug.

I left the store feeling pretty good. I dug my look. This running thing was turning out all right.

RJ and I met the next morning at a nearby high school track for our first training run. It was early, around seven, and neither one of us looked that excited to be doing this.

"Hey," he said.

"Hey," I said.

"Nice shorts," he said. "What are those, like a size forty-two?"

"Let's just do this."

"Hold on," he said.

RJ exhaled slowly and bent over slightly. *Very* slightly. Almost imperceptibly.

"What is that?" I said.

"What?"

"That." I bent over slightly to show him. "What are you doing?"

"Stretching," RJ said. "I don't want to pull anything."

"Pull this. That's not stretching. That's nodding. You look like you're nodding."

"You're right." He straightened up. "Screw it. Let's just run."

We hit the track and started jogging. We huffed and groaned and sweated for a good twenty minutes and then we pulled up. We had made it almost halfway around one lap. Neither of us could catch our breath. We couldn't speak for a long time.

"This was good," I said finally.

RJ held up his hand like he was ordering a beer at a Lakers game. "Great," he said.

At least, I think he said, "Great." What came out of his mouth was a wheezing noise that sounded like "Grrrbrrahahflgmah."

"We gonna do this again tomorrow?" I said.

RJ held his hand up again.

I was pretty sure that meant yes.

He called me that afternoon. "I was thinking. Running a marathon might be pushing it."

"You think? What gave you that idea? Was it that we ran for twenty minutes and barely made it a hundred yards?"

"That had something to do with it, yeah."

"Look, man, we're not kids. And we're a little out of shape."

"A little?"

"Yes. A tad."

"So let's be realistic about this," RJ said. "Let's forget about the marathon."

"Thank you."

"Let's just do the half marathon. Thirteen miles."

"Brilliant," I said. "That'll be much easier."

After training like we were in boot camp every morning for the next two months, we gave up on the half marathon, too. We decided that for our first official race we should go for something a lot shorter: a 5K, which was 3.1 miles. We hadn't been able to make it quite that far yet in our training, but we figured our excitement and adrenaline would push us through the other 2.9 miles we needed to finish.

We signed up for a race in the San Fernando Valley on a mild Saturday morning in October. We showed up that morning along with about two thousand other eager runners. I said something about going back home and sleeping in, but RJ reached over and grabbed the keys before I could start the car up.

"We're doing this," he said.

We got out of the car and found a position twenty or so yards from the starting line. We jogged in place to get loose, and then someone counted down the last few seconds through a megaphone and the crowd started to chant, which scared the hell out of me. It sounded like the running of the bulls. Then the gun went off, scaring me even more, and all two thousand of us runners shouted and surged forward.

Make that 1,998 of us.

"We gotta pace ourselves," RJ said, huffing as we jogged slightly faster than a walk.

"Absolutely," I said, as every other person in the race passed us. "We don't want to burn out too soon."

"Right. Let's slow it down."

"I don't think we can go any slower," I said.

"Tough course," RJ said, bellowing out some air.

"Tough course? We've gone ten feet."

He coughed and shot his hand in the air like he was ordering a beer at a Lakers game.

We plowed forward. Time slowed. We kept pushing ourselves, forcing one leg in front of the other. At one point we looked at each other. RJ seemed to be running first in slow motion, and then in stop-action. I started to laugh and then I realized that I was running right beside him, which meant that I was running in slow motion and stop-action, too.

Somehow—miraculously—we passed the first mile marker. Spectators on the side of the road cheered and ran alongside us, shouting, "You can do it!" and, "You're looking great!" I waved and they applauded.

I don't know how I looked, but I felt like crap. My bottom lip cracked, and sweat poured out of every pore. I made a mental note to go back to that running store after the race, because my nipples felt fine but my dick was starting to chafe.

I thought of picking up the pace, but I was afraid that if I moved any faster, my shorts would fall down. Suddenly, my side started to hurt. I slowed down to slightly more than a walk. I glanced over at RJ. If possible, he looked even worse than I felt.

"How you doing?" I asked him.

He groaned and shook his head miserably.

"Yeah, me, too," I said. "Remind me never to do this again."

"Do . . . you . . . want . . . to . . . *stop?*"

"I don't know. Do you?"

"I don't know. Do you?"

"Do you?"

I looked around. I could see no one else in the race. The road around us was empty, deserted. All 1,998 runners had passed us and were somewhere way ahead of us. We were the last two runners in the race.

"Oh, yeah, oh, *yes.*" RJ held up his hand like he was ordering a beer at a Lakers game.

"What?"

"I think I'm getting a second wind," he said, and then one of us farted.

We both started to laugh.

Then RJ jogged a little faster, challenging me. He grinned at me as he started to pull ahead.

"Hey, what the hell?" I said, pushing out a breath and moving to keep up with him.

Suddenly I heard a clicking noise behind us, as if somebody was hitting the concrete with a stick.

*Click, click, click.*

The clicking came closer.

And closer.

And closer.

*Click.*

*Click.*

*Click.*

"What is that?" I said to RJ.

I turned and saw a blind guy running to the side of us, tapping the road in front of him with his cane.

*Click.*

*Click.*

*Click.*

"It's a blind guy," I said.

"Yeah," he said.

"He's beating us."

"Yeah," RJ said, wheezing.

"He's gonna pass us. A blind guy is smoking us. A *blind* guy."

"I don't think I have anything left in the tank," RJ said. He sounded as if he'd just entered a world of pain.

"RJ, this is the worst. Everybody is beating us. Little children, old people, really old people, and now the sight impaired. With a *cane*."

He grimaced. His face was frozen in one big frown.

"This is embarrassing," I said. "We're not only gonna

finish last; we're gonna finish last behind a sight-impaired person. It's humiliating."

RJ moaned. "I can't help it. I can't go any faster. I'm not sure I'm gonna make it."

"I can't do this," I said.

"You gonna quit?"

"No. I'm gonna tell the blind guy he's going the wrong way."

"What?"

"Just this once. I'm gonna send him over there, toward the mall. He'll be fine. He'll have a good time."

"I want to go on record. This is not a good thing to do."

"I know."

"We may go to hell. Well, you, anyway."

"You're right." I turned to the blind guy. "Excuse me, sir?"

The blind guy turned in our direction. "Yes?"

*Click.*

*Click.*

*Click.*

"Well, see, I want to tell you . . ."

*Click.*

*Click.*

*Click.*

"Yes?"

RJ looked at me. I looked at RJ. I shrugged and turned back toward the blind guy. He kept running, leaning forward. He edged past us, tapping the road in front of him with his cane. He tilted his head toward me. *"Yes?"*

"I wanted to tell you," I said again, "that you're going . . ."

He tilted his head toward me. He grinned.

"Great," I said. "You're going *great*. You're looking good and you're going great."

I gave him the thumbs-up.

"Thanks." He beamed at me and shot past us.

"Running," RJ said after a while, slowing to a walk. I slowed down, too, and began walking next to him. The *click-click-click* of the blind guy's cane echoed off the empty street in the growing distance between us. "This is not for me. If the sight impaired are passing me, I'm out."

"This was a stupid idea," I said.

"Not as stupid as giving him a thumbs-up," RJ said.

"Yeah, well, when you run, you get light-headed and you don't think right. So we're blowing this off, right?" I said.

"Hell, yeah. Blowing off running forever," RJ said.

"Absolutely. Unless we're being chased."

"Exactly."

"Okay, so, cool, I'll just wait here while you get the car."

RJ didn't say anything. He didn't have to. He just waited for me to speak.

"Worth a try," I said.

Next on the list.

"Learn a language."

Finally. Something that I would definitely do. I would like to learn French.

Because the French are assholes, and I want to know what they're saying.

Also it's a prestigious-sounding language, which might impress some people and help me get a better table or hotel room or a better spot in line if I'm waiting to get into somewhere in France that's sophisticated and cosmopolitan, like Euro Disney.

By the way, knowing Spanish does not give you an edge when it comes to learning French. I've been to Paris, and my Spanish didn't help me a bit. I've been to *Spain* and my Spanish didn't help me a bit. I wonder if my Spanish is the problem. Maybe the Spanish I grew up with in the San Fernando Valley is different from the Spanish people speak in fancy places like Spain.

Forget it. I'm changing my mind. No on learning a language. After fifty, it's too hard. In fact, if the idea is to finally do what you've always wanted to do, then what I would do is stay home and watch TV. I not only love watching TV; I'm really good at it. I consider myself an expert, especially when it comes to commercials. You know why?

They lie.

As we've established, I'm the best at spotting a lie.

Let's start with all those beer commercials. They all meld together because they don't make any sense.

It's a hot day in the city. People are leaving work. Guys are wearing jackets and ties, and women are wearing pantsuits and dresses. Everybody's sweating and miserable. All of a sudden a train goes by and somebody pops open a cold beer and the people all freeze and there's ice everywhere. Then music plays and a party starts and there's a deejay and everybody's wearing swimsuits and dancing and drinking beer. Insane. And you know what? I've drunk a lot of beer in my life, and not once has an interracial couple come over and put up a volleyball net. And the Dog Whisperer could work with my dog every day for a month and he'll never train him to fetch me a six-pack.

The stupidest beer commercial is the one where the puppy gets lost. The whole neighborhood rallies around this poor little girl who's lost her puppy, and then everybody goes off to look for the dog. That would never happen. People are so nervous and afraid these days that if you went to the park and asked, "Have you seen my puppy?" every single person in the park would spray you in the face with some stuff. But in the commercial some dude finds the puppy and everybody cheers and another party breaks out and everybody's drinking beer and laughing and the puppy rolls a beer over to a bunch of hot girls in bikinis and the interracial couple is playing volleyball in the pool.

You know who's missing in these commercials? You know who you never see?

Latinos.

We don't exist. We are absent from American life. Apparently we don't drink beer or dance or party or care about a little girl's lost puppy. People from India appear in more commercials than Latinos. It's true. We're getting lapped by people from *India*. The stupid gecko gets more camera time than any Latino actor.

But you know what I do see in these commercials?

Racism.

It's subtle at first, but it becomes obvious if you pay attention.

For example. Every commercial includes one African-American person. Every white guy has at least one African-American friend. Sometimes two. Never more than two, though. They come over. One guy brings milk. The other guy has a cookie. They barbecue and clink beer bottles. Then you go inside and all the guys are watching a game together—three white guys and their one African-American buddy—and they're leaping off the sofa and high-fiving one another and they're all wearing jerseys and eating DiGiorno. Then they make a mess and spill their crap all over and the hard-assed African-American wife makes them all get down on the floor and clean up the carpet, together, as one, in harmony.

The most blatant example of subtle racism I've seen, the one that gets me absolutely crazy, is the commercial for Golden Corral buffet restaurants.

Two couples are in a car driving to dinner. A white couple sits in the front, a black couple in the back. I know. Right. As if. Hang in there. Okay, the white woman starts describing the new high-end restaurant they're going to. She's so excited. She's going on and on about how hard it is to get a reservation. The place is so fabulous and popular and she hopes the new chef is there because he's amazing, blah, blah, blah . . .

Then they pass a Golden Corral restaurant and the black couple in the backseat gets all worked up. They look at each other and grin and then—get this—*they throw themselves out of the car and run over to the Golden Corral restaurant.* Yes. They obviously prefer the inexpensive all-you-can-eat buffet to the exclusive, expensive, fancy restaurant. More their style, I guess, more appropriate. More *them*. So much so that to eat there they will throw themselves out of a moving *car*.

Really?

First, why do the people who make TV commercials insist on creating a world in which white people always hang out with their two black friends?

And second, you know this commercial is fake because in real life, regardless of race, creed, or color, the dudes would be sitting up front and the women in the back.

Okay, I'm glad I got that off my chest.

You know what?

Forget a bucket list. Seriously.

I just clicked away from that Web site.

At fifty, I'm happy just staying right where I am, working, playing golf when I can, and watching TV and sorting my golf tees and ball markers when I need to chill out.

Maybe it's not as exciting as riding a camel, but so what?

It's who I am.

# CONCLUSION
# COMING HOME

**I'M** not gonna lie.

I've had a good life.

Sure, like everyone, I've had my share of ups and downs.

I enjoyed one successful TV series that ran for six years and lasted more than a hundred episodes, and I saw the painful demise of my late-night talk show that flamed out in less than two years.

I survived kidney disease and divorce. One caused me intense and constant pain in my side and nearly took my life. The other was kidney disease.

I met and became friends with some incredible people. I got to play on the same bill with the immortal Carlos Santana, who's become a close friend and spiritual adviser.

I fell in love with golf, traveled all over the country—all over the *world*—and played the most beautiful courses you could ever imagine, sometimes playing with golf legends, such as the incomparable Lee Trevino.

Over the years, golf has taught me some of the most important lessons I've learned in my life, such as to get out of trouble as quickly as you can; don't be a hotshot and make things worse. Golf also taught me how to be patient and persistent when things get tough, and to not be an asshole and let things get to me, and to make sure my clothes match when I leave the house. Also—major lesson—very few people look good in knickers, and I'm not one of them.

I've been fortunate to have earned a good living doing what I love, which is something I wish for everyone. I know what it's like to be poor, and I don't ever want to be poor again, and I don't wish that on anyone.

But sometimes I wonder if I've lost the values my grandparents instilled in me when they raised me in that tract house in the Mission Hills section of L.A.'s San Fernando Valley. I wonder if I've gotten soft.

I started thinking about that house, the one I grew up in, and those days, forty years ago, when I was a kid, trying to figure it out, trying to find my way. Seems so long ago, and yet . . .

There's a trend now that when people go on vacation they want to spend their time living like a "regular person." They don't want to be a tourist. They don't want to stay in a hotel or take in the usual tourist attractions or eat in fancy, touristy restaurants. They want to stay in a typical apartment or bunk with a local family and eat where the locals eat. Sometimes these people even want to get a job for a week or two to really experience the place they've chosen to go on vacation.

To me, that's going too far. If I'm going away on a vacation for the purpose of getting away from work, why would I want to go to work? But people are doing it. Mindless work, too. Stuff like washing dishes, or making up hotel rooms and cleaning bathrooms, or working as an executive at TBS.

But then I thought, you know what, I sort of see their point. Living like a local actually sounds interesting and even challenging. I do think I have gotten spoiled.

I wonder what it would be like to go back to my roots, to my old neighborhood, and live the way I did when I was a kid, when I was poor.

I thought about this one day while I sat having a pot of tea in one of my favorite spots, the comfortable lobby of a famous old Hollywood hotel.

I leaned back in my cushy, overstuffed couch in that hotel lobby and I thought, "How would I do it? Is it insane? Could I disappear for a month and blend in somewhere?"

As I thought about this, a woman wearing a pink polka-dot sundress, a big floppy hat, and oversize sunglasses came out of the lush greenery of the outside patio/restaurant walking her dog on a leash. Yes, this restaurant takes dogs. The woman looked perturbed. She located the hostess, waved at her, then walked up to her and got right in her face.

"We're leaving," the woman said. She nodded at her dog. "Daisy didn't like the food."

"Oh." The hostess, whom I know, looked concerned. "I'm so sorry."

"Well, she ate it, but I can tell she wasn't happy."

I thought, "Sure, she ate it. She's a dog. They eat

anything. They eat dog shit. She probably had the thirty-dollar meat loaf."

"You should've sent it back," the hostess said. "We would have brought you—I mean Daisy—something else."

"Don't worry," the woman said, sniffing the air. "We won't be coming back."

"Wow," I said. "I hope the dog doesn't work for Zagat."

As I watched the woman lead her dog out of the hotel, I thought, "Did I just dream that? This woman was upset because her *dog* didn't like her meal here? Really?"

I decided right then that I needed a break from people who bring their dogs to hotel restaurants and complain about the food. I knew what I would do: I would move into my grandmother's house for a month, alone.

To pull this off, I'd have to make compromises.

First, no cell phone. That meant no texting, no e-mail, no Instagrams, no Twitter, no Facebook, and no apps. No games on my phone, no Draw Me, no Words with Friends, nothing like that.

In fact, no Internet at all.

I would like that.

I know a guy whose Internet went down and his kids went insane. They acted like drug addicts going into withdrawal. They started scratching and hugging each other. They huddled into a corner, holding on to each other tight. Their noses ran and they could barely talk.

"Hey, when's it gonna come back up? How much more of this? How come we haven't gotten it fixed?"

The dad said, "You know what? If this is how you guys are gonna act, maybe I won't get it fixed at all."

*"What?"*

"You heard me. Maybe I won't get the Internet fixed. That way you'll have to learn to read a book."

His daughter glared at him. "That's mean. You're *mean*."

The more I thought about moving into my grandmother's house, the more the idea intrigued me. I wanted to go back in time, when things seemed to be simpler, more basic, and with no frills. Starting with . . .

No smartphone. I would allow myself a landline, an old rotary phone that I would put on a table in the hallway. A basic phone, black, with a plastic neck rest like the one that my grandfather snapped onto it. One phone number, one line. No call waiting and no voice mail. And no annoying answering machine.

I wouldn't take a computer, either. I'd bring a notebook and some pens. If I had an idea, I'd jot it down. Or maybe I'd just let it go. If an idea was worth anything, it would stick with me and still be a good idea a month later.

I would hook up a TV, but I wouldn't get cable or DIRECTV. We never had cable growing up. We got the local stations, channels two through thirteen, and that was it. I'd be able to pick up the Dodgers and the Lakers and, if I timed it right, a big golf tournament. I would miss the movie channels, but if I got lucky, to make up for it, maybe there would be a good high-speed police chase on channel nine.

I would need a car, just in case, but not the Porsche or the Beemer or the Escalade. I'd bring one of the less conspicuous ones. Or maybe I'd go to a used-car lot and pick up some clunker. I'd need something that didn't stand out in the neighborhood and wouldn't get stripped within the first half hour.

As for clothes, I'd pack maybe one bag. Depending on the weather, I'd bring a few changes and an umbrella if I needed one, but I would do my own laundry, so I'd always have plenty of fresh underwear and socks. Oh, and my robe. I can't go anywhere without my robe. I wouldn't send anything out, which means no dry cleaner's. And if I got bored and felt an overwhelming urge to go clothes shopping, I'd have to quash that feeling. No shopping. In fact, I would bring only a small amount of cash. And no black card. I'd leave my black card and my other platinum cards at home.

If I felt like a snack or I needed toothpaste or toilet paper, I'd do what I did as a kid: I'd walk to the gas station. And I would do everything myself. I couldn't send anybody. No assistants. Man, we were talking about totally roughing it.

Wait.

No assistants?

Who would schedule my meetings?

That's right. I don't have meetings.

I could do this. I really could. It would require a lot of sacrifice, but I know I could do it. I'd have to check on one thing before I committed to it: I'd have to make sure that the liquor store near the old house was still there. I always stopped in there after school to pick up a snack. They didn't carry a lot of food, but I could always get some candy or a soda, and they carried a display of my favorite right up front: Slim Jims. And if I rummaged way in the back of their refrigerator foods, I might score the last package of bologna, which was almost like real food.

I think about how kids are set up today and it amazes me. It's so different from how I grew up. They have a pantry full of food, a million choices. I didn't have any choices. We didn't have a pantry. We had a shelf. Now everybody has a little separate room loaded with shelves packed with every kind of food imaginable: breads and cakes and all different kinds of snacks, including ten variations of popcorn—kettle corn, caramel corn, salted, unsalted, popcorn with sugar, hickory-smoked, maple syrup corn, jalapeño corn, you name it—and a variety of chips, cookies, crackers, and drinks, juice boxes, and every type of soda made. In the kitchen they have walk-in refrigerators filled with lunch meats, cheeses, five different kinds of milk, and a million types of yogurt. The freezer is packed with pizza pockets, pita pockets, macaroni and cheese, Klondike bars, Popsicles, Creamsicles, pints of Häagen-Dazs, all sorts of frozen delights.

We had a small refrigerator with a tiny freezer. You'd open the freezer and there was a fish that somebody caught that nobody wanted to eat. No matter how nasty it looked, my grandmother would not throw that fish away. Then you'd poke around and find some tamales from, like, 1972, and some steaks that had turned green and looked like they'd begun to grow legs.

I'd get a job, too. One thing for sure: I wouldn't get the same job I had in high school. I worked at a fish-and-chips restaurant in San Fernando. No way I'd do that again.

My job was to cook the fish, which was a sort of white-fish that we called cod. First, I made the batter. Then I cut the fish, dipped it into the batter, fried it, pulled it out, and served it. My boss, this thin old guy I'll call Joe, would yell at me if I dropped any of the batter on the floor or tossed away the excess. He called the batter the "crispies."

"Hey, you crazy? Don't throw the crispies away. Some customers like it."

If they ordered it, I'd give those customers the bat-ter—just the batter—with no fish in it and charge them half price. I put the plate in front of them, they'd pick up the crispies with their fingers, and I swear I could see their arteries clogging up.

I started the job at the fish-and-chips place the week before I began tenth grade. The first day of school I sat down in homeroom and the kid in front of me said, "Any-body smell anything? It smells like fish in here."

The kid sniffed the air and then he turned around and sniffed me.

"It's you," he said. "You smell like a fish. It's disgust-ing. From now on, I'm calling you Gilligan."

For the rest of the day, every time I said hello to any-body in the hall or in class, they would say, "What's up, Gilligan?" or "How's it going, Skipper?"

After school I went into the fish-and-chips place and found Joe. "I'm quitting," I told him.

"You know what?" Joe said. "You kids all quit."

"Wanna know why? We smell like fish."

"So what? I smell like fish, too."

"Yeah, but you're not in high school."

"The hell with high school. I didn't finish high school and look how I ended up."

That was all he needed to say. I was out of there.

So, yes, I would definitely get a job, but I'd work as a salesclerk. I'd go to work at Walgreens, or maybe Kmart, or Target. Or maybe I could convince the guy at the liquor store to hire me. I'd fill out an application. I'd hope he'd hire me, because then I could walk to work and maybe he'd give me an employee discount. I wouldn't love wearing a uniform, but I'd adjust. That's another thing: Kids don't have to wear uniforms to work. They can dress up any way they want. All the jobs I'm talking about, you need to wear a uniform. I'd like that.

Not only would I do this; I think everybody should. Especially kids. I look back at my life and I feel a lot of gratitude, even for just making it to fifty. I'm not sure that kids understand that concept: gratitude. I know that they're too young to appreciate how good a lot of them have it. I hope that they will someday, way before they turn fifty.

I think it has to do with their parents having a lot of money and not allowing their kids to know what it feels like to *want*. Growing up, I wanted a lot. I wanted to go to places, and I wanted to buy things. I'd ask my grandparents, but they invariably would not give me the stuff I wanted. They weren't trying to be mean or teach me a lesson. They just didn't have the money.

I learned to entertain myself, which I didn't mind. Give me a rubber ball and my baseball glove and I could lose myself for hours.

My baseball glove was my absolute favorite possession. I got it at Kmart, not at Big 5 or some fancy sporting goods store, but it didn't matter, because I knew that when I got through working it, my glove would have the best pocket of any glove in the neighborhood. As soon as I got home with it, I dunked the glove in a bucket of water. Then I put a baseball in the pocket and wrapped one of my belts around the glove as tight as I could. I left it like that overnight. In the morning, I took off the belt, took out the ball, and oiled the pocket with hand lotion. Then I put the glove on and pounded my fist in the pocket—or used the baseball—for an entire week. I never stopped smacking the pocket of my glove. I'd spit in it, rub in the saliva, then bend it, twist it, fold it, put it under the couch and sit on it. Finally, the pocket in that glove was so flexible and so soft that any baseball hit or thrown at me would nestle right in there—*swack*—like it had gone back inside its rawhide womb.

To entertain myself, I'd put on my glove, sit on the couch, which faced the hallway and the closet, and throw a rubber ball against the closet door. It would bounce back to me on the fly. I'd catch it, throw it back, bounce it off, catch it, throw it back, bounce it, catch it, throw it back. For hours. I'd never leave the couch. If I got into a rhythm, I wouldn't even have to change position. I'd barely have to move. Occasionally my grandfather would walk by and I'd nail him in the head. I'd be so focused I wouldn't see him.

*Thwap.*

"Ow!"

"Sorry."

"How many times do I have to tell you? Don't play ball in the house! You're gonna take out an eye."

"Sorry."

But he just shook his head, tossed the ball back to me, kept walking, and I kept playing. . . .

Throw, bounce, catch, throw, bounce, catch . . .

I don't think you could get a kid to even put on a baseball glove today, unless it was a controller and he was waving it at the Wii or PlayStation.

I see parents scheduling their kids all the time, filling up every second of their free time. I don't mean just for summers, but for spring break, too. They send their kids to exotic places all over the world for a week. The parents spend hours on the computer looking for one-week camps, or tours, or internships in places like Hawaii.

We didn't go anywhere. If it got hot, I'd go swimming, which I hated, because I didn't have swimming trunks. I swam in cutoffs. There is nothing worse than when you jump in the pool and just before you hit the water you realize your wallet's in your back pocket and—

*Spplassssh.*

Yes, a lot of kids are spoiled.

I remember when I was a kid playing in the backyard on hot summer days. As the day wore on, I started anticipating the arrival of the ice-cream man. I lived for the ice-cream man. Hearing the sound of that jingle coming down the street made my whole day. But you had to keep your ears open and not get distracted, because you might miss him.

I'd be in the backyard playing ball or something and

I'd hear the jingle of the ice-cream truck in the distance, and I'd stop whatever I was doing.

"It's him! Oh, wait, nah, that's not him. Okay, where were we? How many strikes on you? What's the count? Wait! That is him!"

I'd throw down my glove and ball and race out of the backyard. I'd pull up the latch on the gate and—

*Nooo!*

The latch was stuck!

The gate was jammed. It wouldn't open.

I pulled on the gate with everything I had. I kicked it, yanked it with both hands; it went *thump*; it went *crrrra*; it creaked, scraped, and finally it opened.

I ran out of the backyard to the front of the house, just in time—

To see the back of the ice-cream truck disappearing around the corner.

I'd missed him.

He didn't come every day. If this was Friday, he might not come again until Monday or Tuesday, or maybe he'd blow off our whole street because *the kid who usually buys ice cream didn't show up.*

Yes, I really liked the idea of living in our old house, my grandmother's house. She left it to me. She's been gone now for almost thirteen years.

It's funny: When you turn fifty, you start thinking about things you haven't thought about in years. Moments come rushing back and you start remembering.

Lately, I've been thinking a lot about my grandmother.

When I first started my TV show, I'd go to her house Saturday mornings and she would cook for me. I would sit at the dining room table and read the paper. She'd go into the kitchen and make tortillas, and then she'd cook up some eggs and fry some potatoes and add in some chorizo. She'd put the eggs, potatoes, and chorizo inside a tortilla, fold it up like a napkin, lay a couple on a plate, and bring it to me. She'd sit with me and watch me eat. We wouldn't say anything. When I was almost done, she'd say, "You need any more?"

"Two more," I'd say.

She'd go back into the kitchen and in a little while she'd come back with two more tortillas on my plate. She'd sit down again as I ate them, and after a while she'd ask me, "You need any more?"

"Yeah, just two more," I'd say, and she'd get up again, and then she would get this look on her face, a look of nothing but pure *joy*, and she would go into the kitchen again and in a little while bring out two more tortillas.

We spent every Saturday morning like that, the two of us, just being together. We didn't say much. We didn't have to. We just . . . were. I didn't realize then how special that time was. You don't realize how special something is until it's gone.

I'm not gonna lie: Turning fifty was rough. But at least I made it. And one thing I've learned: Don't look back. Look ahead. And I am. I'm looking forward to moving on with my life and even turning . . . *sixty*? Are you kidding me?

That sounds *really* old. But you know what? I know a

lot of people who've turned sixty and are doing all right. Dr. Phil, for one. He's going stronger than ever. He said that when he turned sixty he realized that three-quarters of his life was probably over, so he decided that he might as well celebrate and have fun. So if there's something you want to do, you'd better get off your ass and do it.

And how about Liam Neeson?

This guy turned sixty and became the number one action hero in the movies. At *sixty*.

That gives me hope.

No, I don't want to become an action hero like Liam Neeson. When I'm sixty, I hope I'm chilling on my couch, watching Liam Neeson on my big-screen TV running around saving his great-grandkids in *Taken 13*. And I'll really enjoy myself because when I'm sixty, he and Dr. Phil will be *seventy*.

But for now, at fifty, I've learned to live in the moment and to enjoy the little things, such as:

- My pantry, which is stocked with everything I like to eat, including a freezer filled with every kind of ice cream I never got to have as a kid, especially when the ice-cream truck passed me by. I think I'll eat a Drumstick or two right now, and I don't care that it's midnight. Actually, I shouldn't have ice cream at all, because when I turned fifty, I became lactose intolerant.

- My new bathtub with the Jacuzzi spray and a side door that opens like a car. I *walk* in, take my Jacuzzi, and *walk* out. Don't tell RJ.

- My size thirty-six jeans. I'm not gonna lie: I can't fit into a size thirty-four, so why kill myself trying? This way, if I overindulge a little, so what? I've allowed plenty of lee-way in the waist.

- My size thirty-eight jeans. In case I was lying about the thirty-sixes.

- Spanx body shapers for men. The greatest invention ever for guys my age, except for maybe the walk-in bathtub.

- My cozy flannel pajamas, my fluffy bathrobe, my compression socks, my new large-print edition smartphone . . .

You know what?
Forget the little things. They're starting to piss me off.
I'm fifty and I'm still here and I'm starting to love it.
You should, too.
Love who you are, where you are, and how old you are.
That's all I got . . .
AND THAT'S THE TRUTH.

# ACKNOWLEDGMENTS

So many people provided wisdom, knowledge, and support during the process of writing this book. I thank you all. In particular, I owe a debt of gratitude to—

Everyone at Penguin Group and Celebra, especially Raymond Garcia, our brilliant and persistent publisher, and Jennifer Schuster, our wonderful editor.

My entertainment and literary agents and management team, who always have my back: Steve Smooke, Christy Haubegger, Nick Nuciforo, Dave Bugliari, Kevin Huvane, Rob Light, Christian Carino, Michael Rotenberg, Richard Abate, Lester Knispel, Rob Marcus, and Inna Shagal.

Ina Treciokas and Charlene Young, my PR mavens at Slate; Linda Small, who runs the Lopez Foundation; and Leslie Kolins-Small, who helms my production company.

# ACKNOWLEDGMENTS

Jim Paratore, my confidant and my brother, who passed away on May 29, 2012.

Dr. George Fischmann, my primary care physician, who keeps me going, especially now that I'm over fifty.

The entire staff at Chateau Marmont, who took care of us and allowed us to hang out for hours during the writing of the book.

My home team, Clarice Amato, Edith Molina, Miguel Meneses, and Carolina Alvarez. You guys are the best.

My close circle of friends, who make me laugh and keep me sane, including my tour manager and buddy, RJ Jaramillo, Bryan Kellen, Ernie Arellano, Arnold Veloz, Anthony Anderson, Don Cheadle, Sandra Bullock, Carlos Santana, Arsenio Hall, Lee Trevino, Eva Longoria, and Jennifer Pryor.

A very special thank-you to Alan Eisenstock. Without him, this book could not have been possible.

Finally, I want to honor the memory of three very special people who continue to inspire me: Freddie Prinze, Richard Pryor, and my grandmother, Benne Gutierrez.